How
To
College

Other Books By Brian Robben

Freedom Mindset

The Golden Resume

How To College

Brian Robben

ISBN-13: 978-1536943962
ISBN-10: 1536943967

DORMS

SCHEDULING CLASSES

ACADEMICS

SOCIAL LIFE

EXTRACURRICULARS

HEALTH AND FITNESS

PRODUCTIVITY

CAREER

PERSONAL DEVELOPMENT

INTRODUCTION

Going to college is about balancing things: classes, homework, social life, student organizations, work, exercise, sleep, finding your career path, and being happy. It's almost impossible to feel accomplished at the end of the day. And it seems impossible to not fall behind. If this balancing act isn't difficult enough, there's no roadmap to navigate it all. There's no guide.

If you're like me, it's not that you don't want to succeed in college. It's that you don't know how.

You want to get good grades, but you don't want to spend your four years studying. You want to have fun, but not go out every night. You want to have it all—the typical college experience that everyone talks about—and get your dream job. So, when it comes down to it, you feel like you have to choose.

But what if you want more out of college? I don't think you have to sell out your future to enjoy college in the now. I don't think you have to choose between college fun or career success.

That's why I wrote this book.

How To College is designed as an all-inclusive guide to solve your college problems. I lay out in-depth strategies for you to get the best grades doing the least amount of work, find the perfect friend group, make the most of your education, eliminate stress, build a knockout resume, and set yourself up for post-grad opportunities. Follow the strategies in this book and you can double as the life of the party and the all-star student.

This book is for anyone before they start or finish college who wants to break free and control their schedule, instead of being controlled by it.

How do I know this? I'll tell you a story about my time in college. On the surface, it looks like I belong in the college hall of fame. I graduated summa cum laude, including a streak of three years where I only received an A or A+ grade. I became president of two student organizations. I started the elite college success website TakeYourSuccess.com during my senior year. And I had countless job offers from top Fortune 500 Companies. (Apparently I couldn't register for the class on humility.)

But I made many mistakes along the way—too many mistakes. I pursued a career in law I had no business pursuing from freshmen to junior year. Before I mastered my study systems, I would study all night without sleep for an 8:30 A.M. exam. Too often I traded fun experiences with my friends to strive for an A+ in my classes instead of an A (what a weirdo, I know). And I even changed my name to Stress Robben—just kidding, but it would have been appropriate.

After being misguided for three years, I put all the pieces together during my senior year. From my personal college experience, interviewing standout college students for TakeYourSuccess.com, and extensive research, I realized that students don't need to choose between a fun college experience and a boring four years paving the way for life after graduation. You could have a blast both during college and after, but only if you did it the right way.

I was blind as a freshman but then I could see as a senior. Finally, I unlocked the code to college success. And I utilized this knowledge my final year of college to study one hour a day for an exam and ace it. I would work on my senior thesis 30 minutes a day and not sweat turning it in. This allowed me to play NHL with my housemates and then go out for Wine Wednesday while still crushing my classes and responsibilities on Thursday.

Now I want to hand over everything I learned to you. Because giving students value, whether it be from TakeYourSuccess.com or this book, is what it's all about for me.

Just as I did, in *How To College* you will discover answers to all of the college questions you have and those you don't know you have. How important is your GPA for grad school and employers? What are the best methods to study for exams and write papers? Is it possible to avoid schedule fatigue and burnout? How do you stay healthy at college surrounded by dining hall food? And how do you make college worth it to find a career you love? Each question deserves your attention, or you risk spending your limited, valuable time the wrong way.

I'm not all talk. Students have already implemented the tactics in this guide to achieve tangible results.

Brittany from Miami University said, "Your study strategies helped me to get A's on all of my finals this past semester. Thanks a lot!"

"You inspired me to change my initial major that I picked based on income (engineering) to pick a major that fits with what I want to do in life (political science). I know it was the right move," said Chris from the University of Florida.

And I receive regular thank-you emails from readers who implemented my tactics and found solid results.

There are 80 college success rules in this book from top-performing college students who've already been in your place. And don't get overwhelmed with the amount of rules, because you don't need to follow every single one to stand out in college.

The truth is there's not one strategy or a three-part system to master college. If there was, this book would be a whole lot shorter. Just as college is complicated, navigating it successfully requires experimenting until you get it right. You'll have to try different puzzle pieces until you find the ones that fit.

I guarantee that if you read and execute the tactics in *How To College*, you'll have more fun and success than you thought possible.

How To College will get you to look in the mirror and ask yourself, "What do I want to accomplish?" and then give you the plan to take action to achieve it. Essentially, you'll go through college living life on your terms.

Read this book straight through or pick and choose rules that apply directly to your situation. The key is that you get started by using *How To College* to make progress. Take action today, with this book in hand, to figure out a study routine, achieve your relationship goals, and land a dream job.

During college, I learned you control the level of success and happiness you experience in life. It's not where you go to school, your past, or tough circumstances that decide your fate. You write your own college story while you're in it, and the strategies in this book will hand you the pencil and eraser to make that story shine. You get to dictate your happiness and become who you want to be in life. So you'll find that many of these concepts are not only college strategies but also life strategies.

I'm so excited for you. And there's no time to waste. Let's learn how to college!

DORMS

Rule #1 - Leave your door open

You might feel nervous about dorm life and meeting people in college. You're away from home and suddenly walking by strangers in the hallway and the community bathroom. Just remember, everyone feels nervous. This is a first for everyone in your hall—you're not the only one.

With this in mind, leave your door open in the residence hall to help others and yourself make friends. It's a small thing you can do to combat those nerves. The only reason your door should be closed is if you're changing clothes or sleeping. This simple move works because you'll immediately be seen as super friendly, even if you're still nervous on the inside.

And this will give others the courage to stop in and introduce themselves. Then when people see a crowd hanging out in your room, they'll stop by in bunches to see what's going on. It's shocking what happens when the barrier of knocking on your door is taken away. Give it a week with your door open and you'll find people who are in your major, share common interests with you, and make friends to spend the rest of the year with.

What's funny is the opposite happens if your dorm door is always closed. You could be the chillest guy or nicest girl, but if your door is always closed, then people notice. And whether they realize it or not, they'll consider you unfriendly and closed off. A harmless decision to close your door for privacy becomes a cold-hearted move in the eyes of people in your dorm.

I'm all for making an effort to get to know people at the recreational center, in classes, in a student organization, and at the bars. But there's no easier way to become popular and make friends than to keep your door open and let people come to you. Then it's not just an open door—it becomes a gateway to lifelong friends.

Rule #2 - Make friends with your RA

A resident adviser (RA) gets a bad rap on college campuses. Students tell horror stories of RAs who are trigger happy to write people up for minor infractions like loud music or breathing too loud after quiet hours. Because of this, the message becomes RAs are out to get you and think the worst of you. And the mentality is it's the RA versus the dorm residents.

I had this same mentality going into my freshman year. Being a rebel, the thought of an RA getting in the way of my fun and freedom pissed me off. But, when I went to my first dorm meeting, I changed my mind about him. He wasn't evil, cruel, or out to get me. He was totally for us and went out of his way at the end of the meeting to offer his advice or service if we needed anything.

I followed up on his offer a few months later and asked him to help me with a job interview for a summer internship. Not only did he send a few pointers, he went above and beyond to send me his resume, a 17-page PowerPoint on job interview strategies, and what he does to prepare.

My RA turned into one of the coolest people I met in college. And by his grace, he saved me from a lot of trouble. One Friday night as an underage freshman drinking in the dorm, I left the pregame room to go to my buddy's room across the hall. The genius in me brought my mixed drink in a solo cup along the way as my RA opened his door and came face to face with me.

I'm thinking it's all over. I'm going to get written up and get an underage citation. He smiles and asks me what I'm doing tonight. We have a casual conversation about weekend plans. But I still think he's just delaying the inevitable and waiting for my guilty confession. Then he tells me, "I need to go to the restroom. Have a nice night!" I walked to my friend's room and looked back to make sure what just happened was real.

And that right there is an example of things that can go your way when you're friends with your RA. If I didn't establish a relationship with him or didn't give him respect, I'm 100% certain I would've been busted for drinking in the dorm.

I also want to bust this common opinion: your RA doesn't want to write you up. They don't get satisfaction or a raise from doing it. It's a pain in the butt and actually more work for them when you consider all the paperwork they have to do. So the thought that your RA gets off on writing people up is a myth.

Be smart by making the school year easier for yourself by befriending your RA. Besides the great resources you gain from them, you could always use the benefit of the doubt when you're on the line or crossing the line. God knows I needed it.

Rule #3 - Manage roommate conflict

Let me state the obvious. Living with someone for the first time is weird. It doesn't matter if they're your best friend from high school or a foreign exchange student you know nothing about—it's still strange.

They're going to have odd habits and quirks that you would never notice if you didn't live with them. Conflict is impossible to avoid when you live with someone (maybe that's why married couples fight so much?). There's no way you're going to live in the same space without any problems.

However, the good news is the way you handle conflict is entirely up to you. And positive conversations where compromises are made will keep the relationship intact, or improve it by strengthening the trust between you two. So getting along with your roommate through the conflicts is absolutely possible. Here's how.

First, establish expectations with your roommate early on to avoid as many conflicts as possible. Talk about what's acceptable when it comes to cleanliness, loud music, other people coming over, and your food in the fridge. Listen to their expectations, but don't be petty. Getting on the same page from day one makes for smoother sailing during the year. But if you wait until there's a problem to communicate expectations and rules, it's usually too late to come to an easy agreement.

And when your roommate does things that get on your nerves, it's in the best interest of both of you to bring it up early. Don't let more than 24 hours go by without having an honest conversation about the issue. Otherwise, you risk letting it boil up inside you along with other complaints until you blow up and have a major screaming match that ruins the relationship forever. Too many students get in the way of their happiness by not addressing the issue with their roommate, and only complaining about it to others. Venting serves a purpose, but never solves the issue.

So when your roommate slams the door each morning on their way to an early class and it wakes you up, insists on putting the A/C at 60°F and you're always freezing, or takes your drinks in the fridge without asking, it's your job to address it soon in a respectful manner before it festers.

Say something that doesn't personally attack them, like, "Hey, it's not a big deal. I want you to do what you need to in the morning. But I'm such a light sleeper, so I'd really appreciate it if you could quietly close the door when you leave in the morning." This takes the attention off of them and puts it on you, so they won't feel attacked and will shut the door softly going forward.

Don't think these tips apply only to freshmen, because they apply to every year you spend at college with roommates or housemates. The last thing you want is to feel like you can't come back to your place and rest after a long day. Your room is supposed to be your safe haven to find peace and get refreshed during the week.

My last advice on this subject is although it would be sweet to be friends with your roommate, sometimes you're just too different for that to happen. And if that's the case, that's ok. Lower the expectations from friend to someone you tolerate and the living situation will go much smoother. Plus, the school year will pass before you know it and bring a new (and hopefully better) roommate.

Rule #4 - Clean five minutes a day

As a college student, you would rather lick a wall or watch paint dry than clean your room. So you leave your clothes covering the floor. Backpacks and notebooks are scattered across half your bed, even when you sleep. And items regularly go missing in the clutter for months.

When you need something and can't find it—a regular occurrence—you waste valuable time looking for missing books, folders, clothes, and shoes. Or when your parents are visiting, you're forced to spend two hours you don't have cleaning your room in preparation.

This time wasted should be used to finish an assignment, hang out with friends, or do something you enjoy. And research has shown that living in clutter can produce stress, impair your ability to process information, and negatively affect your sleep.

You don't want that, and you don't need that in your life. Instead, follow this easy solution: Spend five minutes a day cleaning your room. Implementing this habit eliminates the time-sucking searches for a lost item because you'll be able to find everything the second you need it. And an organized room means you don't ever have to spend two hours doing major clean up because someone is visiting.

Plus, you'll be more at peace, less stressed, and go to sleep quicker thanks to your tidy room. Doing an autopilot activity like cleaning your room creates a space for you to relax each and every day.

The productivity and mental win that comes from organization adds up. So don't underrate having a clean room, because it also plays a part in your college performance.

Rule #5 - Do laundry every other Sunday

This rule probably caught your attention. After all, you wouldn't think when you do your laundry has anything to do with college success. But it does.

A goal of yours should be to mentally automate as many things as you can to save your willpower and energy. This can apply to big things and small things—like laundry. Setting a specific and repeatable time to do laundry (biweekly on Sunday) gives you a mental routine you don't need to think about. This is how you take care of yourself and work efficiently to get the big things done—two things successful students have down pat. If you mentally lock this task in for every other Sunday night, for example, the rest of your college experience you don't need to decide when you're going to do laundry. Isn't that amazing? That's enough reason on its own to do it.

Ok, well when you consider it in a vacuum, saving yourself that decision might not look so beneficial and you might think I'm officially crazy. But when you consider a full day's worth of decisions and willpower, doing something without having to think about it is a blessing. Because your willpower and motivation during a day aren't infinite.

Say you don't put your laundry decision on autopilot and instead decide to address this when you feel like it. So it's Wednesday night and you have a test on Thursday. But oh wait, you don't have any clean pants and realize a monster could be hiding in the mountain of clothes growing out of your hamper. Your mind forecasts to the rest of the week for any openings to do laundry. But then you decide if you push laundry back, you'll be forced to take your exam in underwear tomorrow. Now you're stressed and wish you didn't have to think about this right now.

To avoid embarrassment, you do laundry because it can't wait. But you lose a valuable hour of studying. You also lose some study willpower and focus because of this detour that you can't get back. That lost hour and the weak performance after doing laundry add up to hurt you during the exam the next day.

This is just an example. But setting something like laundry on mental autopilot allows you to always get it done without any hassles. This way you can spend your energy on the activities that matter without interruption and limited willpower.

Doing your laundry every other Sunday is definitely not the most important takeaway from this book. But it adds to the other themes like taking care of yourself and working efficiently. And that can't be understated.

SCHEDULING CLASSES

Rule #6 - Overschedule to drop classes every semester

Bad classes with bad professors are a thorn in the side of below-average students to superstar students. An innocent, blind move to schedule a class you think sounds interesting could turn into your worst nightmare. Common bad course symptoms include working your butt off to only get a C, lifeless course material, or a clashing professor.

All of these make you unhappy and pissed about your class choice.

I'm here to tell you it doesn't have to be that way. You don't have to go through the pressure of pitching a perfect game with your schedule each semester to make sure you take quality courses with excellent (or reasonable) professors.

There's another solution: You register for one or two extra classes, and then drop the worst one(s) before the deadline. Yes, this 100% works since many universities let students drop any course up to a certain deadline early in the semester.

Here's what goes down. Say you normally would schedule five classes, but you're utilizing this strategy so you schedule seven. Go to all seven classes the first week. Get a sense of the professor, their teaching style, the course expectations, and how reasonable the work is based on the syllabus.

This should give you a firm read of what's to come in the rest of the course. Because the boring, old professor who rambles week one isn't suddenly going to turn into a lively comedian in week four. Then you pick the best five classes and drop the other two.

There's only reward and no risk with this stunt. There are no penalties if you drop these extra courses before the deadline. They will never show up on your transcript or affect your grade point average. And your tuition bill isn't any higher since you don't end up taking the extra courses. The only tiny downside is going to seven classes the first week, but it's well worth it when you consider the length of a four month semester.

Gaming the system isn't wrong. It's just making the most of the opportunity presented to you. Do this, and you'll diminish the odds of being in the trainwreck course with the teacher from hell. Now you're learning how to college.

Rule #7 - Check class openings every day

While overscheduling your semester to drop classes is going to make a big difference in your happiness and success, this method has one limit: when a class is full and you can't register for it.

If you've been in college for any time, you know that not everyone gets to schedule their classes at the same time. Usually the students with learning disabilities, the athletes, and the honors students register first. Then it goes by what year you are, senior down to freshman.

After preparing their perfect schedule, students hope and pray registration goes well. They refresh their computer the second the clock turns and click register, only to see the course is already full. Bummer dude!

But don't get too upset, because with a little persistence you can often pull off a mini-miracle to schedule that course. Here's how you can do it.

Almost every student signs up for all the classes they need the first second they're allowed to schedule. But in the months before that next semester starts, things change. These students might change their major, change their minor, transfer, pick up a job, decide to study abroad, or something else comes up.

Any change in their life over these months is often a reason to completely redo their semester class schedule. To do that, they have to drop the courses they're currently registered in and look to pick up new ones that address their new plans.

So the scrappy student (you) takes advantage of this by checking the course registration each day and then looking for it to become available.

I recognize there are other ways to get around the predicament of being locked out of a course's registration, like emailing the professor or showing up to class on the first day of the semester and hoping you're allowed to join the course. But nothing is as clean and easy as registering after someone drops the course and there's an open spot left.

I don't care if you check it once when you wake up or right before you go to bed. But check the class openings once a day to see if you can schedule that last class or two to give you the perfect semester. Do this during the semester before and over winter or summer break.

With this persistence, I transformed my schedule from good to great almost every semester. So there's no reason you can't!

Rule #8 - Take 15 credit hours or less for starters

Some people might tell you to come out of the gates taking 18 credit hours or more in your first semester of college. They think this is best way to graduate on time.

You may have guessed it, but I say it's not the best way! A large semester load when you're new to college can turn into a big mistake. Because the college world is completely different than the high school world. It's like Mars and Earth. You need far more advanced time-management skills to do well in college compared to what you needed in high school. And in high school you could often do minimal work and still get an A in your classes. This isn't the case in college.

This is why I'm against a large semester load for freshmen. When you're dealing with being new to college and taking on more than 15 credit hours, you add more pressure when you're already overwhelmed. And this extra pressure does one of two things.

It either causes procrastination and bad study habits because your classes are out of control. Or you buckle down to keep up with your classes so much that you're forced to neglect adjusting to college. You don't give time to make friends, get involved in an extracurricular, and find your comfort zone on campus.

The general rule is each hour you spend in class requires two to three hours of work out of class. So an increase in 15 hours to 18 hours isn't much on the surface, but this makes for a difference of five to eight hours of homework a week.

Instead, use these five to eight hours to get adjusted to college and develop sound habits: Find the right friend group. Get involved in something on campus. Practice efficient study strategies. Make time to take care of your body and your mind.

When you establish this balance from the start, you'll have what you need to graduate on time and then some. You'll excel in flying colors and have a better college experience for it.

Rule #9 - Don't schedule Friday classes

The happiest students I knew never scheduled Friday classes. So when their last class on Thursday ended, they grew a beaming smile knowing the weekend started and they won't go to class for another three days. When I pulled this off a couple of semesters, man it didn't disappoint.

Of course, Thursday nights are much more enjoyable. You can party without the dreaded thought of making yourself miserable in your Friday morning class. You could also get work done Thursday night and lessen the weekend work. Or you can catch up on something you've been putting off for awhile that you need to get done.

And the secret advantage to no Friday classes is what you do on Friday. Friday is wide open to work on whatever helps you succeed in college. You can take advantage of this free time by preparing for the looming essay due early next week, studying for an upcoming exam, or working a job to pay for tuition. For commuting students, no Friday classes means no need to commute, which saves you time and gas money.

With this schedule, an open Friday is perfect for accomplishing Rule #53 - Pick one day a week to go hard. Put some effort in on Friday during the day and now your Friday night is also wide open to experience the pleasures of college. If you couple your effort on Friday with a strong performance on Saturday and Sunday, you'll be miles ahead of other students all semester.

I recognize that not everyone's schedule allows this set up. Freshmen and sophomores usually don't have the same flexibility in their class schedule as a junior or senior. Sometimes you need to take a certain class that hits on Friday. Other times your major classes always take place on Friday and there's no way around it. But if the opportunity is there to have a little heavier Monday-Tuesday-Wednesday-Thursday schedule with Fridays off, I'm a big believer in going for it.

Remember that if you pull this off, the point is not an entire off-day from schoolwork or work, but an off-day from classes so you have more time to do work and get ahead.

Rule #10 - Add a minor

"Minor schminor, I don't have time for that." This is how many students feel. A minor will provide in-depth learning in a second subject, make them more attractive for employers, and add value to their college experience, but a lot of students think it's too much work. Is this really the case?

In reality, you can add a minor with no consequences. Instead of scheduling two major classes each semester and adding three random electives, you trade the add-on classes for specific classes that fulfill minor requirements. This trade only requires planning in advance, but doesn't require more work or taking more credits to graduate.

So once you pick your minor, bookmark or print out the minor requirements. And when it comes time to schedule classes, do exactly what you do with your major. Plan out how many classes you need to take this semester to fulfill the graduation requirements. You take the same amount of classes. The only difference is you target major and minor classes, instead of only major classes.

If you pick a specific minor during your freshman or sophomore year, completing it is a piece of cake. But if you pick a minor that doesn't share classes with your major, you need to declare it early. And even if you're late to the game in your junior year or early senior year, you're many times not too late if the minor is related to your major. For example, seniors will notice that they can take one or two classes in their final year and pick up a minor (sometimes even another major) that they didn't consider until then. And this is without any planning, just by pure, blind circumstance!

If you're an upperclassman, check your transcript for classes that you've taken multiple courses in and that share classes with your major. Say you're a business student majoring in marketing, it's often easy to add a minor in accounting, finance, or economics. If you're an English major, don't be surprised if you're two classes away from adding a minor in journalism or strategic communications. And if you took a study abroad trip that focused on a subject, I bet you're not far from completing a minor.

So go on and gain specialized knowledge in another field, improve your resume, and get the most out of your education by adding a minor.

Rule #11 - Meet once a semester with your adviser

As a freshman, you're assigned a mandatory meeting with your adviser in the first week or two of the semester. The conversation goes better than expected. You go over your schedule, discuss why you picked those classes, and talk about your major. You learn a lot and gain confidence that you're going to graduate on time. That wasn't so bad!

But then, you never meet with this adviser again. By your sophomore year, you don't remember your adviser's name. And because of this absence, you lose out on an incredible resource at your disposal. Truly one of the only things your college won't charge you for goes untouched. Plus, you risk accidentally missing a major or graduation requirement if you rely on your own planning. If this happens, it always ends bad: summer school, taking 21 credit hours senior year, or an unplanned fifth year.

So don't make college harder than it already is. Just as it's helpful to befriend a professor, the same benefits apply to building a working relationship with an adviser. Think of your adviser as your college wingmate who helps you navigate picking classes, meeting graduation requirements, and learning general college tips. You don't know where the friendship can lead if you don't give it a shot.

But to get the most out of your adviser, you need to be intentional and take charge to schedule times to meet. I recommend meeting with your adviser once a semester. Before the meeting, prepare a list of talking points and questions. Talk about your current schedule and look ahead to some classes you want or need to take in upcoming semesters. Often these advisers are professors in your major who know the most rewarding courses to take and disclose the best professors in their department. And feel free to email your adviser during the semester to tell them how you're doing, see how they are doing, and keep the relationship going.

If you make the effort with your adviser, you'll have inside information to picking classes and getting around college. And when you have another set of eyes checking your graduation requirements, you won't run into any curve balls as you apply for graduation.

Rule #12 - Take a few classes for fun

Of all people to tell you to take a class or two for the fun of it, you wouldn't think it would be me. Especially as I included Rule #66 - Pick one focus and master it, but there's something to be said about spicing up your college coursework with a class or two for the fun of it.

Giving fuel to your intellectual curiosity and taking a course out of your comfort zone is nothing to laugh about. These actions alone are helpful experiences to get in the habit of pursuing. And when you couple that with the idea that college is presumably your last opportunity to have a professor teach you a subject, it makes even more sense. So mix up your schedule with a class you've always been curious about before it's too late.

If you're desperate for examples, try your hand at a photography class. You will gain a newfound appreciation for talented photographers and the detail they put into capturing the perfect lighting. Some of my college friends took a photography course for fun. Then got so enthusiastic about it that they developed their skills and are now professional wedding photographers. Taking photography will also make your Instagram game hot, can't forget about that.

Or take a beginner-level acting class. Getting in a dramatic scene with classmates is a ton of fun and an easy way to make friends. It doesn't hurt that acting class will help you lighten up during the day before your physics lecture.

Others include glassblowing, psychology, art, music, religion, Japanese, or a writing course. But only you know what interests you and what you've thought about trying and decided not to. This time, try the course and see where it takes you.

My only warning is that you confirm beforehand that taking a random class or two won't force you to graduate late. If that's the consequence, then this fun class obviously wouldn't be worth it.

But if you're cleared to do it with no penalty, then learn something you've always wanted to. At best, this fun class could turn into a lifelong hobby or future career. At least, it will refresh your mind during the week and improve your college experience.

Rule #13 - Explore STEM if you're on the fence

With all the time and money (or your parent's money) invested in college, you don't want to waste an opportunity to explore something you're interested in learning about. This is especially true if the subject is difficult, or impossible, to learn after graduation without proper teaching and materials. These subjects basically have a game clock and your time to learn them is running out.

What subjects am I talking about? The science, technology, engineering, and math (STEM) subjects require exploration and advancement before it's too late. These subjects need instruction from experienced professors, detailed labs, expensive machines/tools/programs, and complex problem sets that you can't do on your own. The inconvenience of gaining skills in hard sciences, engineering, and math is absurd if you don't go through the structure of a course.

Because of the specialized instruction and rare resources only a university can offer, it's extremely hard to pursue a career in a STEM subject on your own. That's why if you're on the fence, a wise decision is to explore your interest in this field. Give it a shot before it's too late.

However, you can play catch up with many majors like business, political science, foreign language, English, history, social work, and music. Spend a few hours a day reading or practicing and you can go as far as you want in those subjects. Your knowledge isn't limited to instruction or expensive technology. Often, you can get jobs in these fields without a related major. The same can't be said for the STEM field.

For example, let's pick on my major: English. I know I benefited from some remarkable professors and coursework. But I could have the same writing skills if I didn't spend a day in an English class and only practiced on my own time. Great writers can be made through reading and writing by themselves. While an English or journalism major would help you get a writing job, you could much more easily switch careers from a STEM job to a writing job than the other way around.

So if you're slightly interested about majoring in a STEM subject, take a class or two and see what you think. You likely won't get another opportunity in your life to go in-depth about subjects in science, technology, engineering, and mathematics. College is about exploring, then narrowing in on what you want. And it's hard to know if you want a STEM subject without trying it.

ACADEMICS

Rule #14 - Start strong and coast

What's funny is most college students are convinced the best way to do an assignment is to start at the last possible moment to still finish before it's due. These same people extend this philosophy—to start as late as possible and bear down at the end—to entire courses. And each time they get behind on a research paper, exam preparation, or application, they stress out and give a half-effort. But it gets done, or doesn't, and they continue with this approach.

If only they knew what the top students, and you're about to, know, which is this: the secret to being efficient is to start strong, then you can coast.

Let this visual paint a clear picture for you. The world's fastest man—Usain Bolt—pumps his legs the split-second he hears the gun go off marking the start of the race. And because he put in maximum effort to start the race, around the 70 meters mark he looks left and right to check where he's at. When he sees no one parallel with him, he knows he won the race because no one can catch him from there. So he coasts and celebrates the last 20 meters to the finish line.

Bolt works hard up to the three quarter mark, then he evaluates his progress and his room for error, and then he usually can afford to coast to the finish line and start the celebration early.

Follow Bolt's example by working hard from week one to week 12 and then evaluate your progress. If you follow the other rules in this section, then you should have an A at this point so you can coast to the end of the semester. Many times in college I calculated I could get a D or F on the final exam and still come out with an A in the class because I started the semester strong.

While your peers are having anxiety attacks over finals and calling it the "worst week of their lives," you'll find it as one of the easiest weeks of the entire semester. Just don't be that guy or girl who rubs it in their face too much.

Rule #15 - Put GPA in its place

If you plan on attending a top law school, medical school, or grad school, you better believe that your grade point average is important. Some top schools won't blink at your application if your GPA is under 3.5. Plus, many merit scholarships depend on your GPA in combination with your admissions test score.

The same high GPA standards are present when you're applying for jobs in investment banking, consulting, and accounting. To make the hiring process easier for the firm, they will have hard cutoffs around a 3.5 cumulative grade point average.

But those career paths are few and far between. The typical college student doesn't have Harvard Medical School or Goldman Sachs on their horizon. So why act like it and put in all the energy and stress when your time would be better spent elsewhere?

Take, for example, a graphic design student. Is he better off with a 3.6 GPA and little work experience or a 3.1 GPA and experience as the lead designer for three small businesses? Of course, the latter.

And would an English major be more attractive after writing a book, or spending all semester at the library to make sure they get at least an A- in biology?

What about the college student who plans to make a go of it on her own and start her photography business? She's far better off finding clients and mastering her photography skills than studying to get an A instead of a B in calculus.

The point is this: Relevant and impressive work experience trumps grades for most college students. But I'm not saying grades should be ignored for these students in fields that don't require high grades. Because I would still shoot for at least a 3.0 GPA. Your grade point average can affect how many organization's grant you an interview.

But the fact that you're reading this book and care about your future success leads me to believe that getting a 3.0 GPA won't be too difficult for you. And you can always include your major GPA, if it's higher, on your resume instead of your cumulative GPA.

To wrap it up, if doing well in your future career depends on a high GPA to get you there, then getting As in your classes needs to be a priority. Implement the academic strategies in this book and you'll ace your classes. But if GPA only has a little influence on your future career, then prioritize activities that do help you get to where you want to go and make your grades secondary. You'll be far happier and more successful when you put GPA in its place.

Rule #16 - Go to every class

College students can come up with more excuses not to attend class than they can come up with Kanye West jokes. While I could go on with excuses until Kanye and Kim get a divorce, the main ones include: you don't feel like going, you want more sleep, you have other things to do, you can read the slides online, the professor won't notice, and you don't do anything in class anyway.

It's easy to believe any and all of these excuses, and skip class. However, what's ironic is although it's easy to skip class, your life is much easier if you go to class. And that one reason to go to class trumps all the reasons not to. If you like yourself, then you won't skip classes. Here's why it's so much easier when you get your butt in a seat and listen to your professor.

First, you'll never risk missing crucial information for a project, essay, or exam. Those assignments can be stressful enough on their own when you have all the information. But missing class and key instructions can make doing a project, writing a paper, or studying for an exam one of the most frustrating moments imaginable. It's as painful as attempting a puzzle with missing pieces.

And teachers love to reward students who attend class by finishing a point with the words, "This will be on the exam." When you hear those words, you should be as excited as a dog who hears, "Do you want to go for a walk?" You can make a note to yourself to spend extra time with this concept, and that's something you'd only know because you came to class.

Going to class also gets you access to the information that you don't need to know—which is just as important. Say you're in Biology 111 and your teacher begins a class by saying she's not covering a certain chapter because it won't be on the exam. While the students who missed class waste time studying that chapter, you know not to.

Skipping class often backfires as students waste hours trying to catch up on the material they missed in class or don't need to know. They add stress and anxiety to their life and are more behind than if they had just gone to class.

For all these reasons, don't consider skipping class because you're better off going.

Rule #17 - Write papers in three days or five days

For many students, the truth is that writing a paper feels like going to the dentist as a kid. You have to do it, but you don't want to and the entire process is painful. I don't have a solution for the kid at the dentist, besides get over it or accept bad teeth as an adult. But I do have a solution for the college student facing a paper assignment.

My solution is the exact system I used to earn an A in every writing course I took in college (all 19 of them). Use this system to achieve the same success as me and save yourself any unnecessary stress in the writing process.

To attack big assignments, it's best to cut the work into mini-assignments so you can focus on one task each day without getting overwhelmed. That's the idea behind writing papers in three days or five days. The plan you choose depends on the size of the paper. Follow the schedules below to the tee, and see how writing a paper isn't so bad after all.

The Three-Day Writing Plan goes as follows:

Day 1) Spend 5-15 minutes thinking about the topic and some of your main ideas. Consider what you're going to communicate, and in what order. Then, write out a general idea for the introduction, body paragraphs, and conclusion.

During your initial writing, either start these paragraphs, or write out the main idea and what you're going to write in each paragraph. You want to have enough information and structure that you can quickly pick up where you left off for day two.

If you want to include a full topic sentence, main point, support, and transition for each paragraph, then more power to you. It will certainly help you complete the paper, but isn't necessary.

Day 2) Start on the paragraph that you think will be the easiest. It's smart to start on the easier part rather than the harder section because this way you'll make progress and feel better about the assignment. Momentum is a powerful tool.

Your top priority here is to just get started. Write for two hours and then take a break the rest of the day or night.

Day 3) Write for another two hours and finish what is needed for a complete draft. As you review your work for submission, read it out loud, and fix any holes or awkward parts.

Four hours of prepared, fresh, and focused writing will be enough to ace a small or medium college paper that doesn't require much research.

When you have a research paper or a large term paper due, it's similar to the Three-Day Writing Plan but more drawn out. The Five-Day Writing Plan goes like this:

Day 1) Sit down to collect all your sources and research needed to support your thesis argument. Spending a day to get research out of the way is a better use of time than finding out in the middle of the writing process that you need to do more research. Moments like that kill productivity and can lead to writer's block.

It's also helpful to reflect on the assignment during day one when walking to class, working out, sitting in bed, and whenever you can. Consider what you're going to communicate, and in what order. This will significantly help you the next day.

Day 2) Write an outline with a general idea for the introduction, body paragraphs, and conclusion. Either start these paragraphs, or write out the main idea and what you're going to do when you start writing each section.

You want to have enough information typed out that you can quickly pick up where you left off tomorrow.

Day 3) Start on the paragraph that you think will be the easiest. It's smart to start on the easier part rather than the harder section because this way you'll make progress and feel better about the assignment. Momentum is a powerful tool.

Write for two to three hours and then take a break the rest of the day.

Day 4) Come back fresh and write for another two to three hours to finish what is needed for a complete draft. Review your work, read it out loud, and fix any holes or awkward parts.

Day 5) With the last day before the paper is due, it's important to find feedback. Ask your teacher if they wouldn't mind looking at what you have so far. Or ask a student in the class whose work you respect.

Edit your paper based on their feedback. If you can't find someone to review, then edit your paper yourself. Lastly, before submission, read it out loud and do minor touch ups.

Having a paper writing system in The Three-Day and Five-Day Writing Plan is going to make your writing much more effective and efficient. These schedules offer you the time to do your best work and turn your paper in with confidence. Doesn't that sound good?

Rule #18 - Triple your paper writing productivity

College papers are big, bad bullies compared to high school papers. If they could, the college papers would eat the high school papers for breakfast and take their lunch money.

Rule #17 - Write papers in three days or five days lays out a schedule to write the paper. But sometimes even with a schedule you face a wall that you can't overcome as writer's block gets the best of you. When that happens, you need some countermoves so you can keep writing and get on with life.

As an English major and author, I've written too many words to count. But I can count the best writing productivity tips that help me get off on the right start or correct the course when my productivity has seen better days. Utilize the 12 steps below to write the paper quicker and better.

1) Break your writing into chunks of time in advance: This way the process becomes much more manageable and peaceful. You also get to come back to the paper with a fresh mind.

2) Write at your most productive time: Writing in the morning is usually the most productive time for students. But other students prefer to write at night. If you don't know what time is best, then assume that it's mornings, because that is when you have the most willpower.

3) Write in a quiet place by yourself: Distracted writing leads to procrastination and bad grades. Find a quiet place free of interruptions.

4) Drink, eat, go to the bathroom, and turn off your cellphone before you start writing: The more your body is situated, the easier it is to stay seated and focused to produce more words. And text messages or social media notifications have no place during a productive writing session. The messages will still be there when you're done typing and turn your phone back on.

5) Do your research before writing: Get all the sources, research, facts, and supporting arguments you need before you start writing your paper. Losing your writing momentum because you had to spend 15 minutes searching for a source is a waste of time.

6) Outline your paper: When you outline your writing, your brain gets to focus on following the blueprint instead of overthinking in creation mode. It's easier to lay down the foundation and fill in the concrete than do both at the same time.

7) Separate writing and editing: If you keep editing when you're writing, it will be like taking two steps forward and one step backward. Or one step forward, and two steps backward for some of you. Instead, get comfortable with bad first drafts and recognize you can edit later. Following this one piece of advice will revolutionize your writing productivity.

8) Read the previous paragraphs before you start writing again: This refreshes your mind and gets you back to focusing and creating new ideas based on where you left off.

9) Leave the last sentence left unfinished: By leaving a half sentence and then calling it quits, your mind will be annoyed that the sentence is incomplete. When you come back to it, your brain will immediately want to finish the sentence. And now you've tricked yourself to get off to a fast start writing.

10) Listen to music without words: Playing soft music in the background will give your brain something to block out, which helps focus on the task at hand. Plus, headphones will protect you from personal distraction and present the notion that you're busy to other people who might otherwise interrupt. I've found that lyrics can make it harder to write as your brain is trying to hear words while writing words.

11) Visit your professor or a trusted student to edit your paper: Be polite by asking them if you're on the right track, and sometimes you will get lucky and they will edit the whole paper. It's important to go to office hours or seek help with your paper early, because there's nothing worse than doing major reconstruction after already spending hours writing.

12) Don't write for more than three hours: You'll be frustrated and do more harm than good after that point. A key to successful writing is to be fresh when you sit down.

Rule #19 - Study for exams one week in advance

You might be pissed when you first read this rule and think about studying for a week straight. And maybe that's because your study habits consist of all-nighters, fighting your eyelids to stay open, and procrastinating more than working.

Studying doesn't have to be so bad. I want you to think of studying in a different way, like a normal activity that is necessary, but not torture. And the reason you prepare a week in advance is for the results. But also because this way you don't need to, and shouldn't, study more than three hours a day.

This study system is what I named The Chip Away Strategy. It focuses on breaking down all of the necessary test information into daily, manageable chunks of study time. It's designed to mentally chip away at the exam to improve retention and test performance. It goes as follows:

Day 1) Spend the first day gathering your materials needed for the exam. Don't spend more than one hour doing this activity. The purpose of day one is to get started and build momentum for the rest of the week, not burn out.

Day 2) Transfer your materials into a study guide that covers any possible concept that you could be tested on. This process will help you notice areas where your understanding is foggy, and help your familiarity with the material.

It could be as easy as transferring your notes from a notebook to a stapled packet. Or it could be harder, like if you missed class and need a classmate's notes, or want to add on clarity to your notes.

This will probably be the longest day, but not more than three hours.

Day 3) Focus on the concepts that you don't understand or vaguely remember. If you went through your materials and are not confident you fully understand some ideas, I recommend that you talk to your professor or a classmate that you trust. They will most likely be happy to help.

This preparation could take around two hours.

Day 4, 5, 6) Spend two hours each day doing a comprehensive run through of your study guide. Quiz yourself and speak your answers out loud. The next day, quiz yourself and write down your answers. If you're right, then move on. If you're wrong, then go back until you get it right.

And when you're checking, make sure you fully understand the concept. It's easy to cheat yourself by remembering the answer because you just saw it, rather than grasping the content.

Day 7) I recommend little or no preparation on exam day. If you're nervous and want to be safe, look over the hard concepts that you were unclear about in the beginning of your preparation. You want to go into the exam feeling fresh and confident. Let your preparation take over, because you already put in the work.

I know this strategy works because of my experience and other students who emailed me saying thanks because of their results. For example, a college student named Brittany said, "Your study strategies helped me to get A's on all of my finals this past semester. Thanks a lot!"

So when you have a test coming up, remember to grab your chisel to begin chipping away for the A letter grade. Do test preparation right and you'll eliminate one of the most stressful aspects of college, just like that.

Rule #20 - Actively quiz yourself during test prep

Mulling over the textbook, reading pages of notes, and scrolling through PowerPoints hoping the information downloads in your brain is probably how you studied in high school. Passive studying like this may have worked for you then, but it's going to translate to an above average academic performance at best in college.

The problem with this is passive studying is exactly that—it's passive. And it leaves too much to chance that you're going to recall the information when it's time for the test. Reading doesn't automatically translate to learning, especially if it's late, your brain is tired, and you're zipping through pages. So you never know if you understand the information for the test with this method.

Instead, actively quiz yourself during test prep and then adjust based on what you know. Read the section then pull out the major concepts and rephrase them into questions to answer tomorrow. The next day, attempt each question by actively writing down or speaking in coherent sentences the answers. If you get it absolutely correct, then move on. If it's wrong, mark this question as one to come back to later.

Actively quizzing yourself is the true training grounds for your brain. When your brain is forced to remember information from scratch to write it out or speak it, you'll have a better grasp of what you know and don't know for the exam. Then attack the concepts you don't know until you can quiz yourself and get the answer right from memory. And touch up on the concepts you got right closer to the exam day to make sure they're still clear.

When you combine this active studying strategy with knowing how early in advance to prepare, how long to study for during this time, where to study, and the other test strategies in this book, no test will be too tall of a challenge for you. You've got the entire studying package. All that's left to do is execute.

Rule #21 - Know when to study alone or with others

What do you do when have an exam coming up and your friend says, "Let's study together tonight." You shouldn't immediately say yes because they're your friend or immediately say no because you need to study alone. The answer isn't black and white, it depends on context.

In science classes, courses in the humanities, or other courses where the test is mostly based on memorization, other people can't help you recall the information on test day. So, in general, for exams that require memorization, I recommend studying alone. Or study on your own until you know the information, and then have them quiz you after.

However, studying with others can be extremely beneficial for subjects and exams that require problem-solving, such as math, statistics, finance, accounting, computer science, and engineering.

When students work together in these subjects to discuss homework problems, try different approaches, and explain correct solutions, they can improve their understanding.

Other students will give a different perspective that will help them better conceptualize the information than they could on their own. Or they will learn a more efficient way to solve the problem. Plus, studying with classmates can make the work more engaging, which increases productivity and focus.

Just be careful if you do study with other people. Don't study with people who don't have an exam. Don't study with people who don't have the same exam as you. Don't study with someone you want to flirt with—it doesn't work out well for the exam preparation. And, most importantly, don't study with someone when you have to waste valuable time to explain basic concepts to them because they didn't pay attention or do the homework in advance. (They are leeches who suck the life out of your exam grade). Find students who are as serious about succeeding as you, and you won't have to worry about an anchor who brings down the group.

To summarize, identify if the exam requires heavy memorization or problem-solving. If it's memorization, then you will probably want to study alone. And if it's problem solving, then a group can help you.

Now when your friend says, "Let's study together tonight," you know exactly whether to take them up on their offer or decline based on the course.

Rule #22 - **Never study in your room or bed**

You think to yourself, "Screw it, the library is too far so I'm going to make it easy on myself and study in my dorm room tonight. This move also saves time because I don't have to walk there. I'm a genius."

Not so fast, genius. I can't think of a worse place on college campus to study than your room. (Ok, well if I try then a crowded dance floor at a bar, but you get the figure of speech.) Here's why.

Check out this list of distractions when you study in your room: loud nutjobs across the hall, television, food, video games, roommate constantly walking in and out, roommate's music, roommate talking on their cell phone, and that warm, comfy bed ready to take you in.

Studying in your bed is the devil in this list because your brain associates it with sleep and you'll have a two front war: battling to focus on your homework and battling to not fall for the temptation to go to bed early.

Any and all of these convenient distractions are ready to disrupt your intentions to study by offering you a plate of procrastination. Why torture yourself in this way?

Successful students know there's a time to play hard and a time to work hard. When it's time to work hard, they go to a place where they can focus to get their work done in the least amount of time possible. But your dorm room does the opposite and stretches out what would be a 45-minute reading, for example, into a two and a half hour endeavor. Save yourself the trouble and make your room a "No Study Zone."

Rule #23 - Befriend a few professors

Developing a relationship with your teacher might not be the first thing you think of when your goal is college success, but it pays off to befriend your professor. Here's why.

When your professor knows you're serious about the course and likes you, then it's human nature for them to give you a better grade on subjective assignments. Their opinion of you and your effort can make the difference between you receiving a B+ or A, whether they recognize it or not.

Befriending a professor can also lead to extra benefits at times of desperation. If you build a relationship with your teacher, then you create a better chance that they will be lenient when you need an extension, have to reschedule an exam, or turn in your assignment late.

Professors in your major can help you get an internship or full-time job based on their network. With years spent in an industry, they will have a long list of professional contacts and expert knowledge for students that you can't get on your own.

Knowing the professor well makes for a more interesting class. The same way a class is more fun if you know friends in it, the class is more fun when you've developed a relationship with the college professor. Suddenly, their corny jokes, mannerisms, and way of instructing are considered in a different light.

Lastly, by getting to know your college professor, you can count on a well thought out, personalized, detailed recommendation letter. Many would argue that this is the best advantage for why to befriend your professor since a well-written letter of recommendation is powerful.

Ok, now I hope you're on board. But how do you become friends with professors? That's easier than you think. Professors are real people who have emotions and enjoy when they're appreciated. Knowing that, all you have to do is participate in class, visit office hours, ask about their work, show your appreciation through emails or a quick word after class, ask for their help, and email positive course feedback.

Then when the semester is over, keep the relationship going through updating them about your life. Visit them in office hours a few times each semester to see how they're doing and share what's new. Since almost no students do this, you will quickly become one of their favorite students and unlock the professional advantages that come with that status.

Befriending professors makes your college life easier and proves that nice guys and girls don't finish last.

Rule #24 - Visit office hours often

Office hours can be awkward. They can be painful. And if you feel like you already get too much time with your professor in class, you'd rather put a needle in your eye than meet one-on-one with them. The easy decision is to not spend another second with your professor out of class.

But here's where successful students go against the grain to visit office hours early and often. Top students recognize that going to office hours will help them optimize their time, improve their grades, and help them build a relationship with their professors.

Most professors love when their students are engaged with the material enough to make the extra effort to visit them for clarification on a topic. A teacher appreciates when their students are striving to do great and so they often reward that effort in big ways!

For example, as a sophomore, I remember asking my biology teacher a simple yes or no question about if a certain section would be on the exam. Instead of answering yes or no, he told me all seven main ideas that will be on the exam from that section and what I needed to know about each term.

When the exam came, I flew through those seven questions and thought nothing of it. The next time we had class, everyone around me complained about not knowing any of the terms from this one section on the exam. When I asked what they were talking about, I learned it was the same section that my professor pointed out the seven terms to me earlier that week.

This is one example why the clever students use office hours. They go to understand the most important exam material, get their paper edited, and receive rare insights that go unmentioned in the regular class period.

Knowing this, where's your time better spent when you need information? Is it wiser to spend 30 minutes texting your classmates, searching online, and scanning the textbook for an answer you may never find, or visiting the professor to get a better answer in seconds? The professor is God when it comes to the course, because they designed the assignment, paper, and exam.

And when you do decide to go to office hours, be prepared. Because if you don't have a plan, then you'll likely waste the professor's time and your time.

So schedule a specific day and time in advance by email or speaking with them after a class. Prepare questions about the material to ask them right off the bat. Come a few minutes early to show you're serious and respectful, and avoid pissing them off. Ask the specific questions you prepared and then you can also ask about how they're doing and about their family if it seems right to build a relationship. Send a thank you email for their time. Then repeat this process a week or two later.

Now that you know how going to office hours will make your life easier, you can start working smarter to get better grades and gain more free time.

Rule #25 - Plan and delegate group projects

Here you are cruising through the semester with an A grade average and then the professor mentions an upcoming group project. Now you're flustered. Immediate thoughts rush your mind of being paired with a lazy bum who doesn't do any work, kills the group's productivity, and sabotages the entire group's grade.

You may decide to do all the work to ensure an A grade. But as tempting as this is, it's also painful and takes a significant toll on your time and energy during the week. So there's a better answer for handling group projects, and it's called delegation. When it works, it saves you from spending valuable hours in hero mode.

While you can't force people to do anything no matter how intentional, positive, or charming you are, you can give your best effort to influence other people's performance. And that's often more than enough to thrive in a group project.

From the beginning, say something like this: "Hey guys, this project is a pain, but I need a good grade on this and I'm sure that would help you, too. So let's do our best work and be done with it." Doing this can change the whole mentality of the group moving forward. It sets a strong tone and when you follow up this statement by leading with example in the following steps, the other group members usually jump on board with a solid effort.

Next, just as you would break an exam or paper into smaller tasks, do the same with your group project. Meet the first day the project is assigned to schedule the mini-steps required to go from nothing to finished assignment. By preparing right away, it gives you room for error if you run into problems along the way.

Then get a feel for who is capable of doing what based on their skill and schedule. If Johnny is a graphic design major, have him do the design. If Amanda is an English major, have her do the written report. Delegate what each person needs to do by the end of the week Friday and tell them to email the group with an update. Then meet in person to make sure what needed to be done is done (never trust it is because they said it is) and plan out next week's assignments. This communication sets crystal clear expectations and holds people accountable (with a paper trail from the emails).

Put those three pieces together (set the group tone, prepare in advance, and delegate tasks based on skills) and you'll have a winning group. You'll also eliminate all the stress, frustration, and ignorance from group projects that plague so many college students.

Learning teamwork, how to get the most out of others, and group dynamics are experiences that directly carry over to any line of work you do after graduation. So don't make the mistake of doing an entire group project by yourself, like I've done, and instead be a group whisperer to maximize other people's performance.

Rule #26 - Know when to drop a class

Quitting when things get hard is a terrible habit to develop. And in terms of quitting a class, there are consequences to avoid. But it's not as black and white as this.

Sometimes the best thing you can do for yourself is to withdrawal from a class before it's too late. Dropping a course is a better alternative than putting yourself through unnecessary misery, killing your GPA, losing your scholarship, or other bad outcomes. I know many straight-A students that dropped courses for various reasons, and doing this never ceased to get in the way of their success.

A successful student may laugh at the thought of dropping a class. "I'm better than that," they say. And they might be better. But sometimes things happen that are out of their control and put them in a difficult situation—like a two-week hospital visit.

In these moments, top students recognize when to double down on a class, or when to call it what it is and drop it. They do it by following two requirements.

First, you need to be sure dropping the course won't cause you to graduate late. If you drop a course required for your major or minor, I've seen bad things happen like the course isn't offered until two semesters later, the course is offered at the same time as another required course, or you now have to do summer school and forego an internship. It still might be best to drop it if you failed an exam, but be careful about dropping courses you need for your major. Often they are prerequisites to take other classes and this can throw a wrench in your entire college schedule.

The second and final requirement before it's acceptable to drop a class is that your course fits one of these statements:

- Weed out class for another major

- Professor is a joke

- Work required is unrealistic

- Subject bores you to death

- Class time messes up your schedule

- Took basically the same class in high school

- Failed miserably on the first or second exam

- Missed a long stretch of classes

If you don't need the course to graduate, and one of the above statements represents your situation, then go ahead and quit the class before you're penalized for doing it. When you drop a class under these guidelines, you'll learn the value of addition by subtraction.

SOCIAL LIFE

Rule #27 - Seek the friend group you want

There are so many unique people and groups in college that you don't need to limit yourself by settling for a friend group that you kind of like, or you only hang out with because they live in your dorm. Instead, be intentional to seek the friend group you love. The people who always make you laugh, share common interests with you, and help you when you're down.

To make friends that meet this build, don't overthink it. I find it most helpful to simply be yourself by doing your favorite activity. Then you'll find other people who enjoy the same thing and naturally make friends based off of this common interest.

For example, say you love playing basketball but are struggling to find friends. The first place you should visit is the rec center to start playing pickup basketball games. There you'll meet people who you can play basketball with each week, talk about the NBA, and play NBA 2K together.

Or join a student organization like College Republicans to express your passion for conservative values with other college students. You'll immediately be seen as "one of them" and have friendly faces saying "hi" to you on the walk to class, at parties, and at the library.

And you can increase your success rate by putting yourself out there to meet new people. If you think a guy or girl in your class looks like someone you want to be friends with, ask them to get food or study with you. Everyone needs to eat and study, so this move isn't that risky. To find the friends you want, be proactive. Your task is a lot easier than you think because everyone desires friends, whether they already have friends or not.

These actions aren't scary when you realize that everyone around you is in the same nervous and out-of-place state when it comes to making friends as you, especially as a freshman. They're worried about being lonely, not meeting new people, and not fitting in at college. See, you already have something in common with them.

The worst thing you can do is become so overwhelmed that you stay in your room all day every day, except when you go to class. Being a homebody only makes your friend problem worse and eliminates the possibility of meeting people.

When you seek the friend group you want, you'll not only find friends, but you'll meet the right friend group for you. Investing in friendships makes for a strong social life in college and wild post-grad, reunion parties with your lifelong friends.

Rule #28 - Listen for successful relationships

Look around at a typical college class and you'll see plenty of students who aren't listening to the professor. You'll get the group who is busy texting. The group on social media. And the group browsing their favorite websites (it's obvious that TakeYourSuccess.com is one of them).

This isn't so bad if students miss some lecture points. But, the same happens when class ends and students try to engage in one-on-one conversation. Virtually no one has the patience to actively listen to someone else without multi-tasking. What an outrageous thought, right?

But because people constantly think about their own ideas about a subject, they fail to actively listen and struggle to empathize with the other person. And the unheard speaker feels down about it.

On the other hand, consider how you feel when someone intently listens to you. For one, you feel respected that they listened to your opinion—even if they agree or disagree later on. Two, you'll be more likely to open up. And you will appreciate the listener for being completely present with you.

How does active listening specifically help you? A better question is how does it not help you? When you're establishing a friendship with a professor, active listening builds rapport and shows your interest in getting to know them and their work. When you're settling a conflict with a roommate, active listening is the x-factor that turns a complaint into a quick solution and built trust between you two. When you're interviewing for a competitive internship, making the person across the table feel understood projects a charm about yourself.

And don't get it twisted, active listening doesn't mean you're a mute who doesn't ever speak. It's concentrating on what's being said, processing it fully, and then responding appropriately at the right moment.

I never noticed how good it feels to truly be listened to until I met my friend Graham. When you talk to Graham, his eyes are on you and not his phone or on someone who's walking behind you. And you know what? That feels really good and it opens the door for better conversations.

I asked Graham about this once and he said, "With relationships, I always seek to listen and then speak. I find that most people strongly desire to be heard. They need an outlet for their ideas, feelings, joys, and frustrations. When you listen well, this communicates to your peers that you truly care for them. They will remember this and value your relationship highly."

And although it's not the motive to do it, if you listen well you will gain a long list of people who care for you, support you, and will go to bat for you if anything is needed. This support system makes the bad days ok and the good days feel better.

Rule #29 - Become a great storyteller

Want to be funny and popular? It's as simple as becoming a great storyteller who captures people's subconscious, imagination, and wonder. Your friends and strangers won't be able to get enough of you if you can communicate well. Whether friends ask you "How was that concert?" or "What's your hometown like?" bad storytelling answers with "good" or "boring." Instead, tell them about the anticipation of the first song or what the crowd was like. Tell them about what you and your middle school friends did for fun on Saturdays. This might be obvious, but good storytelling answers with a story—even if that wasn't really the question.

Stories connect the narrator with the audience and the audience with other audience members. Besides being the life of the party and having the ear of everyone everywhere you go, why is this important?

Because candidates in job interviews who tell well-crafted stories go on to get the most coveted jobs. Telling a story about yourself explains who you are and what you want. It also shows the hiring manager you have rich experiences and can communicate it. Hiring managers appreciate stories like everyone else. Storytelling makes such a difference that you can be less qualified and when you tell specific, concrete stories the recruiter will want you more than anyone else. Interviewing is a game and being the best at communicating your skills and resume experiences will be your ace in the hole.

While other applicants who haven't developed this skill will talk about fluff and what they think the recruiter wants to hear, you'll hit the nail on the head and significantly improve your marketability to employers.

To tell an effective story, you need to know your audience and the punchline, have the ending in mind, and get your audience to care from start to finish. The best stories allow the audience to use their senses by visualizing a scene, feeling emotions, and connecting with their beliefs. Showing not telling to let the audience work will keep them engaged.

Great storytellers do all of these things. Good storytellers do some of these, average storytellers do a few, and bad storytellers ramble without a rhyme or reason.

Practicing storytelling is easier than you think. Start by listening to TED Talks, podcasts, and famous speeches. Think of your favorite stories whether they come from movies or books. What captured your mind to care so much and want to keep going? Then practice telling stories to your friends and evaluate the responses you get. If you tell a story or joke and it doesn't go over well, nix it. If you share a story that's well received, use it on other people. Another positive thing about storytelling is you can prepare it in advance, until you don't need to because you'll be able to tell marvelous narratives on the spot.

Rule #30 - Pursue only who you want and who wants you

There are lots of romantic options in college. Since you're young and educated (or getting there), you're also officially hot and people want you. Some students who you see in your residence hall, dining hall, classes, gym, student organizations, and especially those house parties or bars, would do anything to be your man or woman. You got that? You have options all around you.

With that said, many students don't want you. Because they had a bad breakup, are too busy, want to focus on their friends, are shy, don't find you attractive, are dating someone, or whatever, they don't want you. Everyone is not going to like everyone. So you don't have unlimited options.

And this is perfectly ok. Why? I'll say it again: Because you have plenty of options all around you who want you. But for some reason, maybe because it's human nature to want what you can't have, students often spend all of their energy on those who don't want them. They get sucked in this gravitational pull while they get treated like crap, and don't recognize that they're focusing on the wrong person. Don't give your attention to those who don't want you because you'll miss out on meeting the individuals who do want you.

A key to your college love life is focusing on those who want you and bypassing those who don't.

To accomplish this, you'll need to take some risks and face the possibility of rejection. You will need to ask someone for a phone number, to study together, or to hang out. At times, they will say yes and you can spend quality time to get to know if you want them and they want you. Other times, they will flat out say no and that gives you a clear answer.

So don't look at these rejections as failures; they are successes because they bring you one step closer to finding who you want. And these situations far outweigh the sleepless nights, anxiety, and heartbreak from chasing someone who doesn't want you and continues to hook up with other people, or your friends.

And if your college love life feels like it's at a dead end, then get with the times and feel better by hiring a professional cuddler. Just kidding, you're going to be fine and still have your whole life ahead of you to find the one.

Rule #31 - Stand out in one unique skill

Top college students have self respect and confidence. Besides excelling in professional areas, many of them also build confidence by being at the top in an unrelated skill. Compared to their friends, they're the best at playing tennis, singing, drawing, or competing in chess, you name it.

And you have a unique skill, too. This is not your major or career path. It's one unique thing that sets you apart from everyone you know. Usually it comes from hours of practice growing up through high school. Or an activity that you randomly got into and became a stud at it. Think about what this is for you and bring it to college.

How will this help?

Being the best in your circle gives you confidence in your college social life. This confidence translates to trying new things like going on that weekend trip, asking that pretty girl or guy to get ice cream, and signing up for a marathon. Your confidence becomes contagious and translates to other areas of your life.

For example, my high school best friend mastered the game of ping pong. In college, he would look for ping pong tables so he could challenge people and dominate them. He took a ping pong class and always had stories of how bad he beat his opponent or how he talked trash to the professor then destroyed him. Ping pong became "his thing" and what people associated with him. People who were introduced to him would say, "Aren't you the one who is really good at ping pong?" Immediate social benefits all came from standing out in one skill.

So maybe you're the best Madden player. Maybe you have insane magic tricks up your sleeve. Or you can play the guitar at parties. Whatever it is, practice this skill and show if off. It feels good to be known as the best at something, no matter what it is. Enjoy it.

Rule #32 - Stay in touch with your friends and family

With the demanding classes, pressure to make friends, and an uncomfortable new beginning, a college campus is hectic. For this reason, it's easy to get trapped in your university's bubble and receive no air from the outside world. You believe the logical move to navigate your crazy world is to dig in and cut out external distractions. But that often makes the transition worse.

Instead, a better method to handle all these changes is to take a step back and connect with your friends and family from home. Share what's going on in your life (or vent if you're feeling the urge to). I know they would love to hear from you.

Keeping in contact with your high school friends and family gives you a sense of familiarity when that's hard to find. You'll feel encouraged that you're not alone in this, because you have a support system in your friends and family. If you're feeling lonely, one call to a friend or family member can change your entire mood.

Plus, those winter and summer breaks are going to be a lot better with more people to hang out with when you don't ignore your friends from high school during the year.

What fails many students is they believe they need a 60-minute window to talk or it's not worth it. This isn't true. A 10-minute call every now and then can go a long way to sustain the relationship.

And the second danger is only communicating by text or social media. In the past this may have been fine because you saw them on a regular basis. But when you're away at school, a phone call (or video call) is the most efficient way to communicate.

So if you hear something that reminds you of an inside joke, give your friend a call on your walk to class. See an update they post on social media and want to know more information? Ask if you can call them tonight. Little things over time have a big effect.

And I can't fail to mention that if your parents are footing the bill for college, then you have no excuse and you should be ashamed of yourself if you're ignoring them for months. Your family would love to hear from you and it might surprise you that you'll actually enjoy it, too.

Your new college friends are great to have around. But don't forget about your older friendships and family. A support system with your best interest at heart is hard to find. So don't give it up just because you went away to college.

EXTRACURRICULARS

Rule #33 - Get involved, not too involved

There are two students. They are both from the same hometown, went to the same high school, had the same friends going into college, and they have the same major. But one is always excited and inspired throughout the week. The other is lonely and only gets out of the room to eat and go to class. There's only one difference between them. What is it?

The answer is the happy student got involved early on. They're meeting new people, learning the ins and outs of a club, and feeling a part of campus life. They've never been happier and getting involved made the transition to college a breeze.

When you get involved, you meet new friends, find an idea of what extracurriculars are right for you, and what ones are not for you. That's when college is an exciting time to be alive!

So find a club that aligns with your future career like a business frat, pre-law club, or pre-med club.

But don't limit yourself to only professional student organizations. You can sign up to host a weekly radio show, join an intramural sports team, check out a spiritual group, or explore what you love to do. Going once or twice doesn't mean you need to sign your life away. You can never go again if it's not for you.

Go to the meetings alone if you have to and strike up a conversation with the person you sit next to. Or talk with someone on the leadership team and tell them you're new. They will welcome you and most likely introduce you to other people on the leadership team. Then when you go sit down, other people will think you know the leadership team and you're already popular.

Some college rules in this book you can execute a year or two later, but this is not one of them. Don't procrastinate on this. So sign up for something that interests you the first moment you can. Go to the fall student organization fair, or before then, and sign up for one or two organizations.

With all this said, too much of a good thing is a bad thing. So the second worst outcome—after not getting involved in a single thing so you spend your college days bored, alone, and depressed—is being overinvolved. You'll be miserable and feel pulled each and every way by all of your obligations. You won't be able to give your full energy to one group.

Also, having too much on your plate will force you to sacrifice other elements of college success like a social life, sleep, and your health. To the ambitious student who got too involved for the sole purpose of padding their resume and winning at college, this unbalanced schedule will actually be why you're losing.

Rule #34 - Investigate Greek life

Should you go Greek? This is one of the first major choices a college student needs to make. To avoid any blind spots before making a commitment, here are most of the reasons students decide to go Greek and not to go Greek.

Reasons many students go Greek:

- Make friends right away

- Always have social events planned for you every week

- Gain a reliable support system

- Have a strong social status with "cool" friends

- Easy to meet members of the opposite sex

- Plenty of leadership, philanthropy, and networking opportunities

And here are some typical reasons students don't go Greek:

- Prefer free time more than constant social time

- Already struggling with time-management

- The thought of going out at least two nights a week scares them

- Social status isn't a high priority

- They already have a group of friends from high school, their dorm, or an extracurricular

- Money is too tight to afford dues and trips

There are other subjects in this book where I can give a definitive answer, but your decision to go Greek is ultimately up to you. My advice is to get as much information on your own as you can by talking to people and reflecting on if this is a good fit for you. You won't come to a solid decision by sitting in your room thinking about the stereotypes you've heard.

The best way to see if a chapter or Greek life is for you is to be active and investigate. So think of yourself as Sherlock Holmes, because the more information you gather the better. Visit the rush and house nights to get a feel for the people and see if you would enjoy their company. One mistake students make is to assume that the chapter is only evaluating them, and so they forget to evaluate the chapter. Instead, ask the members questions and get an idea of each group's interests and goals.

Discuss the chapters and going Greek altogether with your trusted friends and family. Then based on what you know, make the best decision for you, and go from there. You're going to be fine if you do or don't join a fraternity or sorority.

Because getting involved in a student organization can make for a similar Greek life experience without all the commitment. And keep in mind that being Greek isn't mandatory to make friends and have a great college social life. I attended Miami University, which has the nickname "The Mother of Fraternities" for its rich Greek history, and had a blast even though I wasn't in a fraternity. Like me, you can always join the Greek fun without being an official member.

Life-long friendships and an unbelievable college experience are not exclusive to fraternity and sorority members. So relax and do you—everything else will fall into place.

Rule #35 - Study abroad

College students will hesitate to study abroad for a host of reasons. They mistakenly believe that it costs too much money, only foreign language majors do these trips, and they're missing out on campus life that they'll never get back.

However, in a boxing match between the pros and cons of studying abroad, the pros are boxing champion Muhammad Ali and the cons are your skinny physics professor with chalk on his shirt. There's no comparison!

For one, most study abroad programs cost the same as a normal semester. You pay the same amount for the same number of credits—but your classroom is in Paris, London, Sydney, Tokyo, or wherever you desire!

Two, sure there are programs where you live with a host family to become fluent in their language. But by no means is studying abroad limited to only foreign language majors. There are opportunities abroad for essentially all majors. And if your school doesn't offer one, go on a trip through another university (just make sure the credits transfer).

Point three, don't worry about missing out on campus stuff. Because life will be just like you left it when you come back. Your friends will still like you, and no one will forget about you. But the beautiful thing is you certainly won't be the same. You will have grown, developed, and transformed into a better version of yourself.

Now that we had Muhammad Ali beat up the excuses, there are other benefits of studying abroad as well. The amount of self-discovery that goes on while traveling to different countries is unbelievable. You experience new culture, view different ways of life, and get a global perspective to look at the world. I didn't mention the best part: You will have so much fun and never forget this experience.

And the final reason to go abroad is that a key element of college success is to have no regrets. I'm afraid many adults go through life wishing they studied abroad when they had the chance to in college. They get in the real world and realize it's impossible to find three months abroad, yet alone a week. Their job doesn't allow them to vacation for long enough. Or they get married and have kids that disrupt any travel plans. They ultimately never find a window in their schedule to pull it off.

Don't let that be you. Find out what programs you're interested in based on the location and coursework, meet the application deadlines, and then get ready to go wheels up for the time of your life. I'm excited for you!

Rule #36 - Only work part-time jobs with extra benefits

It's smart to work a part-time job in addition to taking classes when you need money to pay for tuition, housing, food, or alcohol. And even if you don't need the money, hustling to increase your standard of living or build wealth is commendable. However, there's a crucial difference in working any job and working a job that offers you extra benefits.

The first ideas floating in a student's brain are the normal jobs: dining hall cashier, restaurant server, bookstore staffer, or barista. They're accessible and easy to find. Here's my advice: Don't work these kinds of jobs because they offer no extra benefits in addition to the paycheck. They often stress you out or leave you with less energy for the rest of the day. And since the money is about the same at any part-time job, it only makes sense to find work that helps you succeed in college or figure out what you want to do in your life. These jobs will pay you the same—sometimes significantly more—and they provide free time to do homework or direction in your future career.

Easy desk jobs that ask little of your attention are perfect part-time work. Being an office assistant, receptionist, or library front desk worker offers you the quiet free time to do hours of homework. You get paid to knock off assignments! You might get interrupted here and there to answer a phone call or check out a book, but the vast majority of time is open to write a paper, study, or get other work done. That's a winning part-time job.

The other favorable option is to get a job related to your career so you can discover if it's for you or not. When you think you want to become a chemist, work in a lab with a professor. If you want to become a professor, work as a TA. If you're considering medical school, get a position in the local hospital or campus health center. These jobs not only pay, but they also tell you if you're on the right career track. If you love that line of work, you now have contacts and information to help you get into grad school or land a job. If you don't enjoy it, you know you need to switch direction, and or switch your major—before it's too late.

Attaching a purpose to your work beyond money will motivate you instead of sucking your energy like other jobs. As a barista, you're always on call so you can't study for an exam or make progress on finding what you want to do after graduation. This limitation is frustrating when other work does provide those perks.

Successful students get the most out of everything, including their work. So assist yourself by working a part-time job with benefits. This job will become another resource in your arsenal for how to college.

Rule #37 - Commit to community service

To pad their high school resume for college admissions, serve others, or a little bit of both, many students come into college with some experience in community service. But in college, little attention is given to volunteering when juggling academic, social, and extracurricular responsibilities. And that's a shame.

You see, the number one reason to volunteer is to help others by giving your energy and time. Knowing that you're responsible for changing people's lives who are less fortunate than you will infect you with positive emotions. When you make a difference to put food on a table or build a house, it's a reminder that you're not too small to completely change people's reality. You also realize that there are people nearby who you can serve, so you don't have to wait for a service trip to Africa.

And for those who want to become social workers, teachers, psychologists, counselors, or other social-related work, there's no better way to get experience interacting with a diverse group of people than local community service. These community interactions will help widen your perspective and worldview.

Serving is an activity where you go to help others and come back convinced that these people helped you. It's easy to become self-centered in college and get overwhelmed at everything going on, but serving is a way to release this pressure. And since many habits are formed in college that stick with you the rest of your life, volunteering is a powerful habit to practice.

So join a service student organization, propose that your student organization volunteers to serve the community, or volunteer on your own. There are many programs dedicated to service, which often include delivering food, building a shelter, tutoring low-income students, or fund-raising.

Students who go on to make big differences in the world later in life, first learned that they can make small differences right now. Give volunteering a try if you're skeptical. I have a feeling you're going to love the effect it has on other people and yourself.

Rule #38 - Become a student organization president

When it comes to student organizations, here's an average student's mindset: I'll join this business group, engineering club, sailing club, and this service group. My resume is going to be sick. Now I look like The Most Interesting Man In The World.

In reality, I would say, "What are you talking about? Your resume is going to suck." There's no way to be actively engaged in four clubs. You'll be busy and maybe make a few meetings for each student organization, but you won't go any further than that.

Then, when a recruiter asks about a club during a job interview, like, "I see you were in this engineering club. What did you do there?" And the honest answer is that you only went one time to get free pizza, it's going to suck—like I said. Not to mention you look like you don't know what you want to do in your life when you sign up for four different organizations and can't speak in depth about any of them.

Instead, I highly recommend you break through the noise and gain leadership experience in one student organization. Because this experience carries more value for employers than a long list of memberships to extracurricular organizations. To break it down, you get more with less in this case.

If you have solid time-management and organization skills, you can certainly do this job and learn as you go. Don't let self-doubt get in your way.

It's not as hard as it's cracked up to be to lead a student organization. You have a team of leaders with their own responsibilities, an adviser to go to in times of need, and general members who are often helpful in giving solid feedback. My team often worked much harder than me in their specific roles, and I only managed the team and general body members.

And the fact that many students fear running a student organization and think it's too hard is to your advantage. There is less competition running for president than there is secretary or treasurer. Everyone thinks they can be secretary or treasurer, not president.

So find one student org where you want to be president. Attend every meeting. Volunteer at events where the executive board needs help. Talk to the current president and ask their advice on how to follow in their footsteps. Do everything you can to show your interest and commitment to that organization, and then become president.

And when it's time to apply to organizations or grad schools, this leadership experience will serve you well compared to the majority of applicants without it. For example, I remember a Deloitte recruiter saying he valued my president position above my 3.97 GPA. This same guy said he values leadership experience above all else when evaluating candidates.

And it's not all business. Leading a student organization will also reward you for stepping up to be in charge. While it's easier to sit back at student organization meetings, or not go at all, the satisfaction in life comes from action in those moments—in speaking up, raising your hand, and getting involved. Easy things in life are boring, while challenges are interesting. That's why learning how to bring in quality speakers, plan trips, recruit new members, and navigating the organization will be compelling.

Plus, if you're only a member of a student organization, you might make a couple of friends that you say hello to and sit by during the meetings. But if you're president, this is a whole different story. Because you share common interests and goals with these people already, you'll make friends with your executive team, general body members, and prospective members who want to join. An unengaged general body member might make two to three friends, but a president of a student org will make 10 to 20 new friends almost by default.

Rule #39 - Get your writing published

How do you know you don't love writing if you've never done it for yourself? I don't doubt you've written many papers in English class and other courses. But that's not what I'm talking about. Because if you've only written under the constraints of an assignment and a professor's expectations, you're writing in chains. I'm talking about writing to express yourself and to encourage dialogue about a topic that's interesting to you.

Writing because you have to and writing because you want to are two different worlds. Many college students cannot get enough of writing for fun. Sharing their voice on subjects important to them is empowering and boosts their self-esteem. There's nothing to complain about in this arena.

And there are plenty of areas to publish your writing: the student newspaper, the local newspaper, a literary magazine, an academic journal, or a blog. These publications are always looking for new content.

If you're looking for the easiest barrier to entry, the student newspaper's Opinion section is your best bet. This section consists of opinion pieces and commentaries which don't require writers to be a part of the staff. You want to do your best on spelling and grammar, but don't worry if your writing isn't up to Shakespeare's level. I'd recommend getting a friend or an English professor to do a quick read through, and then submit it.

You'll find it's rather fun to construct an argument about something controversial to get other students' attention. And often times other students will write a response to your piece to continue the conversation.

So are you passionate about freeing the orcas in SeaWorld? Are you upset *The Wolf of Wall Street* glorifies criminals? Do you think the American political system is nuts? Sit down at your computer, or grab a drink first, and write about what you believe (just make sure you have someone edit it before submitting when you drink and write).

Once you get published, I won't be surprised if you want to write another piece. Or if you enjoy it, join the student newspaper team to get your own regular column.

Rule #40 - Apply for scholarships every semester

Getting checks for $500, $1,000, and $2,500 for scholarships is one of the best feelings in the world. But only a few students experience it. Why's that? It's because most people think it sounds too good to be true.

For one, scholarships are not only awarded for academic achievement. You could also get scholarships for living in a certain county, pursuing a certain career path, and being related to an employee at a company.

And here's the hidden secret behind winning scholarships: Almost nobody applies because they assume other people are more qualified so they won't win. For you, this means if you do apply and follow the application instructions carefully, you already put yourself in a position to win because the competition is smaller.

To find the right scholarships, start by speaking with professors in your department. Through the cooler talk or internal emails they will be the first to know about relevant scholarships and awards. Talk to your university's career services office and your advisor to check out what information they might have. Another idea is to ask your siblings, parents, and parents' friends if their company sponsors college scholarships. And if you're in a fraternity or sorority, then checkout the national office's scholarship awards.

Don't waste your time going to a scholarship site like fastweb.com, because then you're competing against hundreds of thousands of college students. It becomes a lottery that you'll never win. By getting off of Google search to email or speak in person with real people, you shortcut your way to winning scholarships.

This free money is appealing enough to apply for scholarships every semester. And we haven't discussed the kicker. The bonus is that these scholarships will tune up your resume for applying to grad school or the job search. Winning these awards helps you advance in your career, and has the potential to not only pay you in the short-term but also improve your chances at a higher salary or grad school scholarships.

With the clear benefits of free money and a noticeable resume boost, spending a few hours each semester to apply for scholarships is an easy decision. May the odds of winning the free money and accolades be ever in your favor.

Rule #41 - Don't transfer without a legitimate reason

Transferring happens, but the devil is in the details of why you want to transfer. Switching schools because you're uncomfortable and want to run away from your problems is not a logical solution or habit you want to start. I'm sorry that you had a bad breakup, didn't get into your number one fraternity or sorority, or are having trouble making friends. Those situations are hard. But none of these are legitimate reasons to transfer. Because every college is going to feel uncomfortable at times.

And how do you know you're going to be any happier transferring? What if you're just as unhappy, then do you transfer a second time? What if the problem is you and not a single university? Plus, the way you're going to be happy at a new college is the same way you're going to be happy at your current one—by putting yourself out there.

If you're reason for transferring is because you're going through a bad season, then I think a better solution is to change your approach. Seek the friend group you want, get involved in a student organization, and be patient. If you do put in the effort and patience, but your gut still says something is off, maybe it's time to transfer. Just make sure you have a legitimate reason the new university is a better fit.

Legitimate reasons to transfer include your university not having a major you need to specialize in for your career, tuition is too expensive, not offering specific social things you desire, or other inadequacies. You need to be able to hit the nail on the head for why you're transferring and how the new university is better able to address your need, otherwise I wouldn't transfer.

If you do have a legitimate reason to transfer, the next hurdle is finding a university that also accepts all of your credits—or close to it. You can recover if the new university doesn't accept a class or two. But if transferring to the new school puts you a semester, year, or further behind on graduating, don't do it. You will only get rid of one problem and add a worse one, like going to college for six years.

Transferring can be messy, so don't take it lightly. That's why when you don't have a legitimate reason to transfer, the best move is to stick it out at your current university and be patient that things will improve. With a legitimate reason, you know what to look for in your next university and you're positive that the problem isn't you.

HEALTH AND FITNESS

Rule #42 - Eat healthy, eat for energy

An endless meal plan and the freedom to eat whatever you want whenever you want seems like love at first sight. That's until you find out your plan isn't perfect, and comes with a lot of baggage that negatively affects your body and college success.

The weight gain itself is frightening to your health and happiness. Stack enough dining hall buffet plates of onion rings, fries, and ice cream on top of each other, and the freshman 15 is an understatement. What's more likely to happen is the freshman 30. But it gets worse.

The true killer that accompanies unhealthy foods is the sluggish feeling that never goes away. This diet jeopardizes attempts at focusing during lecture, doing homework, and having energy for your social life. Since it takes your energy without discriminating, you'll have less energy for everything. That's why eating unhealthy is essentially attaching a weight to your ankles in every aspect of college. And college is already challenging, why handicap yourself?

To be direct, filling your body with unhealthy crap turns your body and mind into an unhealthy piece of crap. It can only use what you put in.

However, students who eat healthy give their body rocket fuel to excel in their classes, extracurricular activities, and workouts. These high energy levels help them get more done in two days than students who eat unhealthy get done in a week.

I don't expect you to suddenly eat like an Olympian athlete. Just make small changes and you'll see a difference in your daily energy level. Eat eggs instead of Pop-Tarts. Go for a chicken Caesar salad instead of McDonald's. Drink water instead of soda. And party with vodka soda instead of pina coladas.

Taking care of yourself is worth it. If you respect your body by eating healthy, it won't let you down.

Rule #43 - Learn how to cook

It's unbelievable to me that students can become proficient in a major like nuclear physics, break apart a computer and put it back together again, and get a job offer from a top military defense contractor. But these same students will also go through college not knowing one of the most fundamental life skills of all: how to cook. They can construct a rocket ship, but are clueless when it comes to making pasta. How does that make any sense?

These students aren't missing anything in their classroom, but they are missing out in the kitchen. Because knowing how to cook is a healthy and useful life skill that will serve you more than a butler in a mansion. The single best way to eat healthy and improve your quality of life is to cook for yourself. And you'll need to provide for yourself when you graduate, so don't delay the inevitable. Learn how to cook now when you have more free time on your hands (trust me you'll have more free time in college than in the real world).

If you're worried about cooking taking too much time out of your day, I found that cooking actually saves a lot of time. Because you don't need to walk out of the way on campus to find food. You avoid all the lines in the cafeteria or off-campus restaurant. And if you have a couple of quick meals in your repertoire, you can cook it faster than the campus chef's or restaurants. There goes that excuse.

Frozen pizza dinners and microwavable sesame chicken meals are easy to make, but these choices bring a hefty price to your energy levels, weight, and health status. So get yourself a pan, saucepan, spatula, and chef's knife. Start reading about basic nutrition, experiment with Pinterest recipes, and begin with easy meals until you work your way up.

Soon you'll be making vegetable omelets, salmon salads, and tilapia tacos. Cooking healthy is not hard if you make a small effort to learn and try. Then invite your friends over to eat, and they'll be obsessed with you for giving them a break from the tiresome cafeteria food.

Each time you learn a new skill and empower yourself in college, like cooking in the kitchen, college will feel more comfortable and exciting. And you tell me who is more attractive: A nuclear physicist, or a nuclear physicist who can cook and has a rocking body because of it?

Rule #44 - Work out at least every other day

I hope you didn't get the intention that achieving college success is a lazy cake-walk requiring no effort. It's difficult to motivate yourself to do something and then consistently execute, but that's the fun in it—when you overcome the struggle. And one area where many college students lack motivation and discipline is exercise.

Anyone can hit the gym two weeks before spring break out of fear that they don't look like a beached whale. But it's a different story when you're challenged to work out regularly. Any sliver of doubt when it comes to not having enough time or not feeling like it will destroy your exercise plans for the day. This can turn into a cold streak where you don't exercise for an entire week, month, or semester.

What's the solution? Set up barriers and create a habit. Just as you breathe air without thinking about it, get yourself to work out without thinking about it. Figure out a way to work out at least every other day.

In this order, here's what you do. Find an accountability partner—a roommate, friend, someone you know who works out—and make a commitment that you both won't let the other one down by skipping an exercise day. Then compare your schedules to find what 60-minute time slot works best. Once you decide on a day and time, stick with it.

Since humans are creatures of habit, just get started and let yourself follow the routine. If you can get in a solid rhythm working out, your energy and motivation levels will be at an all-time high. Energy plus motivation are the ingredients to power you to accomplish everything you need to and more during your college career. Basically you'll turn into Superman!

Exercise also releases happy hormones in your brain. It's why you feel euphoria on your way out of the gym. That's the reason anytime you're feeling down or depressed, the first thing I recommend to feel better is exercise.

Not only will regular exercising do all these things in college and more—like improve your confidence—you also build a habit that will serve you the rest of your adult life. Getting in a consistent exercise routine is bigger than winning at college. It helps you win at life by taking care of your most important assets: your body and mind.

Rule #45 - Drink half your body weight in ounces of water daily

Do you know why scientists consider dolphins one of the smartest animals in the world? I'll tell you why. It's because they drink so much water that their mind stays sharp and energy stays high.

Now I have a confession. The part about dolphins being smart is accurate. The explanation why is a complete lie.

It's true that drinking water throughout the day will increase your energy and keep your mind focused. Since around 60% of our bodies are made of water, we need water to function. And a hydrated body feels energized all day, doesn't make random trips to get snacks, and suffers less headaches.

Dehydration leads to feeling sluggish, which leads to procrastination, eating out of boredom, which leads to interrupted study time plus unwanted weight, and frequent headaches, which damages your focus.

So start drinking half your body weight in ounces each day. If you weigh 180 pounds, then drink 90 ounces of water each day. This may seem like a lot, but it's doable with a couple moves.

To achieve this goal each day, I've found the best solution is to carry a water bottle with you everywhere you go. Seeing it during class or carrying it on a walk to the library will remind you to drink more water. It's also helpful to drink two large glasses of water for breakfast, lunch, and dinner. You'll find the easiest time to consume water is when eating.

With this amount of water intake, the only potential downside is you'll visit the bathroom often. But that's ok, because you can fit this time in during your study breaks.

Rule #46 - Sleep seven to eight hours a night

You can hit snooze as many times as you want to squeeze in every bit of sleep before class. If your first class is in the afternoon, then no one is going to stop you from sleeping for 11 hours. Even if you have morning classes, you can skip class in favor of more quality time with your pillow.

But do you want to spend a large portion of your college years sleeping and feeling tired? Or do you want to have enough energy to make it through each day?

If you want to get the most out of your college experience, trade in the snooze button and oversleeping for getting just enough sleep to feel rested and energized all day. Hit the sweet spot of seven to eight hours of quality sleep. You need it because during this time, your brain is making connections to learn and remember information. Your brain and body are also recharging for optimal performance the next day.

Connor, a successful student at Cornell, highlights the importance of sleep in his life, "I sleep about eight hours a night. Sleep is incredibly important to my productivity because without it, I tend to lack the motivation to get work done unless it's due immediately. I tend to procrastinate when I'm tired and this trend turns into a counterproductive cycle that just causes more stress than is necessary. If I am well rested, I am much better at staying on top of my assignments and avoiding late nights doing schoolwork."

When you combine working out and eating healthy with adequate sleep, your mind and body will operate at a high level.

Rule #47 - Sleep like a baby

No one wants to mess with insomnia. Maybe the most frustrating thing in the world is going to bed with the intention to sleep, only to waste two hours telling your brain to turn off in between counting sheep. You also pay for it the next day with daytime sleepiness and poor academic performance.

How uncool is that? You're not out of luck though. Tweak your sleep routine a bit and you can go to bed right when your head hits the pillow, and wake up feeling rested and happy.

Achieving better sleep starts with going to bed and waking up at a consistent time each day. If you do this, you train your body's clock to naturally sleep through the night and to wake up on time. You will start to wake up a minute before your alarm clock, and when you get good you won't need an alarm.

Next, at least 30 minutes before bed, turn off your phone, laptop, and other electronics. Otherwise, the bright screen tricks your brain to stay energized right up to the point when you try to go to bed. This causes insomnia because the brain needs time to unwind. It's not a light switch.

And since you won't have your phone or laptop before bed, try reading or journaling to clear your mind by reflecting on the day. Replay your day to process how it went, what's coming up, and how you're feeling. Going through this process relaxes your mind and gives it permission to rest into sleep.

You can take other steps to prevent insomnia, like exercising during the day, designating your bed only for sleep, avoiding naps, not drinking caffeine or alcohol at night, and having a pitch black room, but those three sleep tips above are the most important.

When you have no trouble going to bed and waking up, your productivity, mood, and quality of life increases. Sleeping like a baby is a blessing in college.

Rule #48 - Keep sadness in perspective

The phrase "college is the best time of your life" will be thrown around by everyone. A phrase like this sounds clear, simple, and innocent. It's encouraging students to get the most of their experience.

On one day, you'll be on cloud nine, and they will be right that "college is the best time of your life." But what that phrase fails to mention is that the next day, college will completely defeat your spirit.

For example, maybe you don't get into the fraternity or sorority you wanted. Maybe you fail an exam. Maybe you're homesick. Maybe you're overwhelmed with classes. College can crush you into a pool of sadness.

To make matters worse, maybe you're struggling in an area it seems everyone else is excelling. Say your best friend got into their number one fraternity or sorority. Or your roommate has a 4.0 grade point average. Everyone else loves being away from their family and the freedom this offers. All your friends are having an easy time with their classes. And you get the vibe that you're the only one feeling this way. Your self-talk says, "What's wrong with me? Everyone else is having more fun than me."

Knowing that these are supposed to be the happiest years of your life makes your sadness that much worse. The phrase "college is the best time of your life" might be true for your friends, but it feels like a punch to your stomach when you're already down.

This is when you need to give yourself a break. You didn't do anything wrong, you're just going through a rough patch and that's ok. You're down, but you're not out. Your life isn't going downhill with no return.

In these moments, don't isolate and fall for the social media trap that everyone's life is better than yours. They're struggling and confused at times too, you just don't know it. At one time or another, everyone else is having doubts about this whole "college is best time of your life" thing.

Instead, discuss how you're feeling with a friend, significant other, or family member. Open up about how you're feeling, because venting on its own will help you. And what helps the most is hearing that other people are also struggling and confused. Knowing you're not alone in feeling this way will keep the fact that you're only having a bad day or week in perspective. Soon this sadness will pass and your days will get better.

And, I think these moments of ups and downs are what makes college so great in the end. It's not all perfect, but you learn a lot in the less-than-perfect moments.

With this mindset and support system, you can weather the college storms and appreciate the happy moments because you know how you feel when you're down. Keeping sadness in perspective isn't often thought of when pursuing college success, but it should be.

Rule #49 - Practice positive thinking

"Be positive" is a cliché that's often the last thing you want to hear when you're upset about something. Can't you just see your mom saying, "Be positive and it will work out honey. I just know it?" Too bad your problems are real, you think, and that advice is poop.

Except science also says your mom is exactly right when it comes to positive thinking. When you have positive thoughts, your brain can change itself to form new habits and increase performance. So how you think influences your life.

And researchers have found that positive people find more success and happiness. This is because they're thinking positive, so they learn new skills, then they achieve success, which leads to more happiness, and then the cycle repeats.

This isn't magic, witchcraft, or voodoo. I used positive thinking many times during college to take action and achieve real results. And I found during the times I didn't practice positive thinking, I slumped hard and couldn't climb out of a rut.

What's behind this simple truth to "be positive" are colossal results.

Take, for example, interviewing for an internship. If you go into it with negative thoughts that you're unqualified and there's no chance you're going to get a job offer, your thoughts will come out in your preparation, body language, facial expressions, and answers. Negative thoughts cause a poor interview. On the other hand, say you come into the interview feeling positive about the opportunity. You visualize getting the position before you interview. This confidence will empower you to outperform more qualified candidates in what you say and how you say it. Internal thoughts create a different reality!

Or take the looming group project. Will it go better and be more enjoyable if you have a positive outlook of learning from other people? Or a negative outlook where you're convinced your group is worthless because you could do it better by yourself?

Assuming you're now a believer, there are a few ways to practice positive thinking. It all begins with being grateful. Think of a few things, big or small, you're grateful for each morning. It's impossible to be negative when you're in that mental state. Then visualize having a productive and favorable day. If hardship comes, recognize it as an opportunity to learn and improve going forward. It always helps to surround yourself with other positive people. Sometimes this means stepping away from negative complainers. Do this daily until it becomes a habit.

Listen to Buddha, who said it straight and true, "All that we are is the result of what we have thought. The mind is everything. What we think we become." Practicing positive thinking will bring real value to you and your college days. The only hoax is on people who don't practice positivity themselves.

Rule #50 - Find your stress release activity

Confused students believe college is a sprint where they need to go, go, go at all times. They can hardly keep everything they need to do straight in their mind, let alone accomplish it all. And when too many activities pile up, stress comes knocking right behind it to cause damage.

Some stress puts you in a bad mood. Significant stress can cause depression.

College isn't a sprint, it's a marathon. And you can achieve a ton in college, but not if you get burnt out. So the way to stay fresh is find your stress release activity and once a week let yourself get away from it all. Leave all the students, campus noise, and college-related stress.

To do this, go on a morning run. Hike at a nearby park and surround yourself in nature. Find a nook in a local library to get lost in a book. Doing something off campus and being by yourself are the goals here.

During this time, take a break from thinking of your upcoming exams, looming group project, friend drama, and summer internship search. Give yourself permission to release any stress because when you come back from your escape, it will be there waiting for you.

Finding your stress release activity isn't a miracle worker. It won't clear your busy schedule. But it will give you more energy and freedom to tackle your schedule. And that's what matters. A stress release activity reminds you that you run your schedule, it doesn't run you.

With a few of these activities in your pocket, you have an outlet when you start to feel overwhelmed. Doing this to recharge, even if it's only for half an hour, will help you tackle that busy schedule.

PRODUCTIVITY

Rule #51 - Make a priorities list every semester

An average college student juggles any of these responsibilities: classes, social life, job, student organizations, exercise, community service, intramural sports, and more. It's exhausting to think about it. But it's even worse when it's real and you feel you have to balance all of these activities at once.

Demanding schedules like these can quickly turn your life into a mess because each day you're stretched out and blindly guessing where to devote your time. Sometimes you get it right and everything goes smooth.

But usually you devote too much time to one responsibility and then suffer in all the others. The balancing scale tips too far and you don't know how to fix it.

A nursing student at the University of Virginia, Nicole, has a solution, "One tangible time-management tip that has worked for me is to make a priorities list. At the beginning of each semester, I write down all of the things I'm involved in and then I prioritize them."

Nicole continued to say, "Once I have done this, throughout the semester, I look at what I'm spending the majority of my time doing and evaluate whether or not it aligns with my list. If it doesn't, then I either readjust my time commitments or I consider changing my priorities list."

This time-management tip is perfect because it holds you accountable to make sure where you spend your time aligns with your priorities.

If you're constantly reminded that your number one priority is to find a summer internship, for example, you know you can't fit five intramural sports teams in your schedule. If you don't have the priorities list, those five intramural sports are going to look appealing and the internship search will take a backseat—if you don't forget about it.

Plus, when two commitments conflict, which happens more often than you realize, you know what one trumps the other and deserves your time.

Just as the Magic Mirror in *Snow White and the Seven Dwarfs* never lies, your priorities list never lies when it tells you how well you're balancing your time. So let your priorities list guide your time-management and you'll fly straight to where you want to go.

Rule #52 - Begin the day with your most important task

You'll hear this a lot in college: "I'm so busy." Students will moan all of the time about how busy they are. In college, everyone is busy, but telling people you are busy becomes a social status. Saying "I'm busy" symbols success and importance.

Here's the thing: Anyone can be busy. Anyone can go from morning to night like a chicken with their head cut off doing a lot, but getting little done. You can be busy reading emails. You can be busy color coding your study guide. None of these busy activities are the best use of your time. So if you want to win at college, the goal isn't to be busy.

Truly successful college students realize it's easy to be busy, but better to be productive. And the most productive thing you can do to start your day is to prioritize your most important task first.

If you're a junior going to medical school, start each day by studying for the MCAT. If you're a senior looking for a consulting job, spend the first hour of each day practicing case study interviews and reaching out to your network for connections.

I don't know what your most important task is, that's for you to decide. What I do know are the benefits of accomplishing this each day.

When you knock off that activity first, you'll feel an emotional high that stays with you the entire day. It's the same feeling as when you leave the gym with a rush of endorphins. And who doesn't want to feel like that every morning?

Achieving this will also propel you to overcome the rest of the day's responsibilities. The confidence from completing this difficult work in the morning will give you momentum that will make your other work feel like child's play.

But here's the ace. By doing your most important activity in the morning, you're making strides toward accomplishing your big goals for the future.

On the other hand, pushing back the big things on your to-do list for night time will make you dread the whole day. And choosing to do busy work—like send emails and check your syllabus—will leave you farther from your goals and feeling overwhelmed. You have less willpower at night, so you risk procrastinating on what needs to get done because you spent all day doing less important tasks.

The best way to beat procrastination is to not give it a chance from the start. So screw the petty activities that might make you feel productive but that don't need to be done. And cut out time for your most important activity in the morning. Taking steps closer to your future dreams, while building a powerful habit for life, is what college success is all about!

Rule #53 - Pick one day a week to go hard

No one wants to experience bad things in their life, especially if it's repeated week after week. And one of the worst experiences in college is the feeling of struggling in your classes. This often happens when students face multiple exams in the same week, projects and papers lining up back to back, or sometimes a normal week with demanding classes. There seems no answer to fit it all in unless you decide to drop sleep for 72 hours straight—but that's a flawed plan that destroys your health and leads to awful performance.

The reason there's no viable answer is students wait too long and let the week get ahead of them, instead of getting ahead of the week. A solution to limit this overwhelmed feeling in your life is to clear an entire morning or afternoon once a week to get ahead of your schoolwork.

The day you go hard can be any day, however this works better on days where you don't have class. Saturday or Sunday are the best fit for most students. Or if you follow Rule #9 - Don't schedule Friday classes, then Friday is an attractive option.

A Fulbright Award winning student describes what he does, "To balance schoolwork, I take full advantage of Saturdays. I am a firm believer that one can have a ton of fun each night of the weekend but still get up by 10 or 11 A.M. to head to the library. I never once studied on a Friday or Saturday night during my entire undergraduate career and achieved an overall 3.76 GPA. On Saturdays, I consistently put in four to six back-to-back hours of work in the quiet university library. This allows me to stay on top of work and often to keep ahead. I hate feeling like I am drowning in work by Wednesday morning and having a solid study session on Saturday mitigates this mid-week overwhelming feeling."

When you work extremely hard one day a week, Monday morning isn't so bad because you feel positive about being ahead of your studies. And you're not exhausted by the end of the week because you've been a day or two ahead all week.

Another benefit is this solution also enhances your time to play. You have the flexibility to drive an hour away to try a new fish taco spot or you can go to the bar on a random weeknight to watch a game without worrying that your grades are going to tank. This peaceful flexibility flows smoothly because you didn't backload your work for the night before.

Create this habit and you will think the students who are overwhelmed with their courses speak a different language than you.

Rule #54 - Use temptation bundling to beat procrastination

A creative solution to make what you should do more enjoyable and feel guilt-free about what you want to do is through temptation bundling.

Temptation bundling means combining one thing you should do but struggle to finish, with some other action you want to do but isn't productive.

Many students motivate themselves by attaching negative consequences if they don't study for an exam, work out, or visit office hours. For example, you might think you'll fail a class if you don't study or you might think you'll gain weight if you don't work out. This way of thinking is "I'm going to do this, so I can avoid this bad thing." If avoiding the negative outcome is the only motivation to do it, it's not all that motivating.

Instead of that approach, try something called temptation bundling.

The difference is that temptation bundling joins two activities. You decide on an activity you really want to do—like watching a movie or getting ice cream with friends—but, you can't do that until you've finished another, more productive activity—like studying or washing the dishes. Working this way improves your motivation because you're not motivated out of avoiding negative consequences, but motivated from a positive reward system of doing the second activity. This mindset ends up being more successful, because you're not acting out of fear. And, in case you haven't noticed, fear is often demotivating. A type of motivation built on rewards or positivity is powerful.

You can also use temptation bundling to do the two activities at the same time. You'll feel more enjoyment out of both activities when doing them together than you would if you did them separately.

What does this look like? It comes in all shapes and sizes. Promise yourself a feast at your favorite restaurant after you block off two hours to study. Only allow yourself to watch Netflix when you're on the elliptical. Bundle applying to three summer internships before day drinking on Saturday.

If you keep doing this, you'll take the fear away from getting stuff done. When you have a desirable activity to look forward to, you'll likely complete the first activity. When you reward yourself with the second activity you want to do, it's the perfect temptation bundling. Procrastination won't have a hold on your willpower after implementing this tactic.

Rule #55 - Abolish all-nighters

Misguided college students will walk into their exam room and tell anyone who will listen, "I pulled an all-nighter last night. It sucked, but I got it done, bro."

They treat their all-nighter like a badge of honor where against all odds they stormed the castle and slayed the dragon. Here's what actually happened.

After throwing back Red Bulls and eating candy bars until 2 A.M., their brain is fried. Their ability to learn new information is nearly gone and only worsens as they go on. Their eyes are now glazed by 5 A.M. and they're not retaining any information from the PowerPoint slides they click through in rapid succession.

As the night turns into the morning, their caffeine high has faded to a hangover and their brain has morphed into smush. And then they ask this depleted and dysfunctional brain to perform well on their exam in 10 minutes.

But, you know how the story ends. Their all-nighter ends up being the reason they perform so poorly on the exam. By trying to do whatever possible for their exam, they actually self-sabotage their grade.

And that's not the only consequence. Now their fried brain is forced to go to class or do homework. This brain brings terrible results, like missing class and putting aside work all day to take a six hour nap. These decisions lead to stress and anxiety the rest of the week. Remember, this all snowballed from the all-nighter.

Now that you know the problem of the all-nighter, this is why students resort to it. It's not an overwhelming schedule that forces students into pulling all-nighters. It's their lack of planning mixed with procrastination.

So remember that the college student who embarks on the all-nighter is not a hero, but a fool. Pity the fool who pulls all-nighters.

Rule #56 - Use a timer when studying

Although Eckhart Tolle didn't have studying in mind when he said, "Awareness is the greatest agent of change," he could have. Because students who aren't aware of how much they actually study in a sitting, will blind themselves from the reality and feel more prepared than they are. But when they're aware of how much, or little, they studied for, they optimize their studying for a more productive day.

How do you become more aware? Use a timer each time you sit down to study.

This tactic involves a couple of steps:

1) Set a goal of how long you're going to study and then start a timer that counts down from this number.

2) You have to stop the timer every time you lose focus and get distracted. So if you stop studying to check your phone, browse social media, go to the bathroom, or talk to your friend who walked by, you stop the timer. This is the most important step.

3) The last rule is you can't stop studying for the day until your timer hits 00:00.

This works so well because the sobering experience of knowing how much studying you actually got done will motivate you to focus and set distractions aside. There's no way to get around it unless you completely lie to yourself—but then you have other issues.

For example, if you've been sitting at the library from 7:30 to 8:30 P.M. and your timer shows you only studied for 23 minutes, you will be motivated to focus so you can move on to something else sooner.

If you don't do this timer-method, then it's easy to convince yourself that you got most of your work done since you've been here since 7:30 P.M. You fool yourself into thinking you put in the necessary effort to do decent on the exam, until the exam— which holds everyone honest—exposes your study flaws.

It's helpful to have others keep you accountable, but nothing is more important than you holding yourself accountable. So set that timer and concentrate until your time runs out.

You'll perform better on your exams and get more out of your day this way.

Rule #57 - Work in 48 minute increments

How do you eat an elephant? One bite at a time is the answer. But a better answer is one bite at a time in 48 minute increments with 12 minute breaks in between each feeding frenzy.

In seriousness, top students don't eat elephants. But they do work smart by studying in 48 minute chunks every hour. They set a timer for 48 minutes and work nonstop in complete concentration until the time's up. Then they take a break for 12 minutes to go to the bathroom, drink coffee, and relax their brain. After these 12 minutes are up, they set the timer for 48 minutes and repeat this process.

It seems random and odd—especially if you're used to going to the library at 9 P.M. and studying until 3 A.M. without any structure or breaks—so you might ask why does this work so well? The reason it's so effective is because setting a goal to study for 48 minutes gives your brain a concrete task to focus on, and this inspires action.

For example, instead of sitting in a blank stare feeling mad that you have to read six chapters by tomorrow and you can't get started, your brain will focus on the short-term goal of reading for 48 minutes. Then you take a break and come back to the work with the positive realization that it's not so much work after all. You've already made solid progress. Then you can build on this positive momentum and structure to knock out more chapters.

So the 48 minute structure is a short-term goal that helps you stay on track and focus on what's important in the moment. And it's better than being productive for 10 minutes and then taking an hour break.

And don't underrate these 12 minute break times. They're just as important and the secret sauce to this method. Because taking breaks allows your brain to get re-energized and refocused for future performance. The gravy is that these breaks help your mind retain information and make valuable connections.

You couldn't draw up a more effective work scheme. When you study with this schedule, your results will surprise you. You may wonder why you haven't always worked this way.

Rule #58 - Use a two-method time-management system

Time management is critical for college success and survival. If you don't already know this, you'll soon figure it out. With so much riding on how you manage your time, you can't leave it to chance. You need a plan.

What worked for me when managing classes, student organization president responsibilities, a job, workouts, and more, is a two-method system between a planner and a daily to-do list. Use a calendar to write in assignment due dates on a weekly and monthly timetable. Then write in your daily tasks on a post-it note that you attach to the left or right of your laptop keypad.

Spend 5 to 10 minutes thinking about what needs to be done tomorrow, and how important each task is to accomplish your weekly and monthly assignments. Then write down these daily tasks in the order of their importance. The next day, finish at least three tasks. Then, you get to do my favorite activity: cross them off your list! Repeat this process every day. Add the less important tasks that you don't finish onto your post-it note the next day, until they become more imminent and climb up in priority. Or if they're never a top priority, they may never get done and that's ok.

When you make a plan the night before, you give yourself a head start when you wake up the next morning. By using this strategy, you're not going to waste time thinking of what you're going to do and when you're going to do it. Plus, you will accomplish your most important tasks first, and then see what else you have time for.

The concept is similar to how runners put their running outfit and shoes by their bed at night, so in the morning they can instantly put them on and go outside to run. Limiting decision making will give you more energy and time to get your tasks done. The more experienced you get, the better you can fine-tune your to-do list and productivity over time.

Rule #59 - Create intermediate deadlines

It's easy to complete small assignments. You break down what you need to do, and you do it. But when it comes to large assignments due weeks later, something switches in your brain and you get intimidated. Suddenly, you're stuck in procrastination mode.

A key contributor to procrastination on large assignments is your brain feels overwhelmed and anxious with all the work required. The assignment feels so far away that there's no urgency to work on it until weeks later. This leads to not working on the assignment until it's so late you have no choice to do it or you won't finish in time.

What's the solution? Create intermediate deadlines by breaking your large assignment into smaller assignments—what you are naturally better at. This eases the pressure of the big assignment and adds urgency. And when progress is made on a smaller assignment, this gives you motivation going forward. Instead of rushing to throw stuff together, you can take your time and do your best work.

Here's how it works in an example. Let's say your geology group project requires a PowerPoint presentation in front of the class on the history of the national parks and it's due in two weeks. You create intermediate deadlines to give two days for each of the following tasks: general research of the national parks, find three main points to focus on, collect statistics and sources to back up your points, add the information to the PowerPoint, practice your presentation, and make last minute edits. Now you have seven mini assignments for two days each. These assignments aren't intimidating, they require work each day from now until the project due date, and you build positive momentum as you go to finish without stressing last minute.

This method works for everything: papers, tests, group projects, internship applications, student organization fundraisers, and more. Execute your schedule this way and you'll never give the procrastination monster life to ruin your productivity and peace.

Rule #60 - Don't binge-watch

We've all done it right? We get lost binge-watching our show, episode after episode, until we see our face on the screen and come to the sobering realization that we haven't moved for hours.

Don't get me started on the laziness. But that's the least of our worries here. You don't learn about yourself in this zoned-out state. You don't get outside your comfort zone to meet new friends or try things you'll never get the chance to once you graduate. And it often leads to loneliness and depression.

Think about it. Have you ever binge-watched something, gotten up, and said, "Wow, that was time well spent. I feel on top of the world!" Probably not. Instead, you say to yourself feeling ashamed, "I'm a useless bum."

You wonder where the time went and stress about unfinished homework due tomorrow. You wish you were intentional and spent that time hanging out with your friends. Or you dread waking up tomorrow morning at 7 A.M. after going to bed at 3 A.M.

I'm not saying that you can't watch Netflix an hour a day here and there. What I'm saying is that I'm convinced your college performance and personal happiness decreases the more you binge-watch shows. So why go down that road?

The only exception is if you watch a series with your friends. This is different because it's social where you build camaraderie off this shared interest. That leads to inside jokes and more importantly developing friendships, which is a principle of college success.

But if you're prone to watch endless hours by yourself, save yourself the time and do something that will make you feel happy. Exercise, chill with your friends, read a book, or play sand volleyball. No one has ever looked back on their college experience and wished they watched more of their favorite show. You won't either.

Rule #61 - Schedule specific free time activities

Depending on your personality, there are two sides to the coin of free time. The workaholic-type will say free time isn't free because it costs valuable time for their to-do list. On the other hand, the procrastinator loves free time too much. They will allow a one hour break to play a game of Madden turn into a three hour recess and three games of Madden.

Whichever one you are, you're doing it wrong if you're not getting any free time or you're getting too much free time. Free time is important to unwind and relax during the day as long as you don't overdo it. And when you keep a healthy relationship with free time, it actually boosts your daily productivity.

The normal recommendation to make time during the day to relax is to schedule your free time. Compared to not scheduling any free time at all or overdoing it, this solution works. But it has some holes in it. The biggest hole is that it's easy to see this time as flexible to keep working on something you deem more important. There's not much structure, which makes it less likely for you to do it.

That's why there's a more advanced solution: schedule a specific activity for free time. Go a step further to reflect on what you want to do during your free time and lock it in your schedule. For example, if you know you're going to take a one hour break after lunch, schedule a tennis match with your friend. Or decide you're going to watch the baseball game for an hour.

Doing this also protects against wasting your free time laying on the floor staring at the wall in boredom only to be disappointed when the time is up and you didn't utilize it well.

When you schedule a specific activity that you like, treat it like something you have to do such as writing a paper or studying for an exam.

Implement this tip and you won't have the guilt of being unproductive while you're enjoying yourself. Because you're being productive. You'll feel refreshed getting "you time" in during a busy schedule. By scheduling free time, you can now enjoy the best of both worlds when you're in working mode and relaxing mode.

Rule #62 - Reward yourself every week

We've all seen the hamster running on the wheel attempting to catch the cheese. But you've never envied its position and said, "I want my life to look like that." Of course not, that would be a ridiculous thing to say. The hamster is in this uncomfortable state but keeps going and only gets slower as time passes.

Unfortunately, too many college students find themselves as the hamster and their school work as the wheel. For example, they go through a tough week of taking three exams, submitting multiple internship applications, and writing one paper, that takes a toll on them. Then they stumble onto the next week and never feel refreshed. As each week rolls on, they feel less motivated and less happy.

But it doesn't need to be this way. Instead of going through college like a zombie, give yourself a reward after every week. This simple solution works wonders to keep your mind fresh and motivated for the next week. Give your brain time to de-stress and unwind, and you'll stay mentally healthy the entire semester.

Before you object that you don't have the money or time, don't overthink the idea of rewarding yourself. I'm not talking about jetting to New York City for a weekend filled with massages, shopping sprees, and lavish meals. Many successful students reward themselves in a small way and still achieve the goal. You could order breakfast in bed. Or you could treat yourself to a day trip without thinking about any work. The more creative you get with it, the better.

"I believe in the motto 'Work hard, Play hard.' I worked hard during the school week and then rewarded myself by relaxing with friends on the weekend," said a college standout named Yousra.

She explained her mentality further, "Sometimes, all that kept me going was the idea of hanging out with friends or FaceTiming my family, and it made me work that much harder to get to the weekend and breathe that final sigh of relief."

Knowing you have some time off on the weekend to relax is the perfect motivator for efficient work during the week and protects your motivation going forward by keeping your brain fresh. As some say, "treat yo self!" You'll find more success because of it.

Rule #63 - Drink coffee every day

I used to hate coffee throughout high school, until I tried it again my freshman year. Even then it tasted gross. But man, the boost in energy and performance made me feel like a sucker for not drinking it earlier. After that initial week, I discovered that students who drink coffee have an advantage. (I also find it delicious—an acquired taste.)

In college, you'll have some late nights and early mornings and some Sunday afternoons where you feel like napping. What's one way to overcome all of that? Coffee. Coffee primes your productivity by heightening your brain activity and your focus. The ability to concentrate at a high level allows you to retain more information in one hour than the student without caffeine who studies for three hours to learn the same information.

Essentially coffee drinkers are better equipped to win in college because coffee affects their brain causing them to be happier, more motivated, and more productive. For this reason they outperform those who don't drink coffee and have more time to enjoy college life.

Not only that, but coffee is a social thing in college. You can meet people standing in line for coffee or meet up to study at a coffee shop.

Besides supporting your college success, coffee also has other positive effects. One is that coffee can be beneficial for your liver. You know the organ you beat up during your college career if you consume large amounts of one particular liquid?

Although coffee can help you feel energized in the morning after a night of little sleep, don't make this positive effect a negative by drinking it before bed to mess up your sleep schedule. This would do more harm than help. So don't drink coffee too late in the evening. Drink coffee on top of a good night's rest and you'll be on fire.

Thanks to illegal steroids, Barry Bonds set Major League Baseball's single season homerun record. Thanks to legal coffee, you can set your college's single semester productivity record.

So have it fully loaded with cream and sugar, have it flavored, or have it black, just make sure you get your cups of coffee in during the morning and afternoon. Your brain and your body will thank you.

CAREER

Rule #64 - Treat college like the start of your professional career

In middle school and high school your parents ran the show and decided your path. But in college, it's up to you. And no one can direct your career path better than the person you see in front of a mirror—not your parents, advisors, or society, so don't let them. If you do, you risk settling for a career that never fulfilled you in the first place.

Going to college will help you learn subjects, become self aware, and make friends, but it won't pick the right career for you. Because you're the captain of the ship now, college is the start of your professional career. You choose your classes and your major, which opens up and eliminates many careers.

That means the stakes are high from the beginning. And what you spend your time on continues to carry more weight each year for your professional career. So don't wait to follow your curiosities and experiment in fields you might love until your junior or senior year. By then, you're too late for many opportunities. Get after it right away.

Start reading about careers, take challenging classes, join student organizations that interest you, and get internships (even work for free). Taking action will give you confirmation in what you do and don't want to pursue.

Then once you find something that sticks, gain a collection of relevant experiences in that industry to put yourself in the best position to get a full-time job offer.

People who come out of the gate with the perspective that their professional career starts in college are more inclined to find what they want to do and achieve it. Those who don't do this are the type who change their major senior year, graduate late, and don't get the job they want out of school.

It's okay to explore different things in college, but make sure you keep your future in mind. In simple terms, there are no do overs in college.

Rule #65 - Follow your curiosity, instead of a major

Initially I thought a book on college success needs to address how to pick a major. But after serious reflection, I decided that I can do one better. I can help you find what you're curious about. Because finding a major and then looking for what you want to do for your career is backwards.

Instead, start with your curiosity and then pair it with a major. Doing it in this order leads to enjoyment and success because each step, even when it's hard, is more fun if you're already curious. Suddenly you're talking with your teacher after class because you want to learn more. Or you're raising your hand and asking questions during the lecture to go even deeper about the subject.

To follow your curiosity, start gathering information about it. Read about it, talk to others, shadow professionals in that field, and think about whether you would enjoy this career. Take small steps and see where it leads you.

And you don't have to worry about not knowing what you want to do after graduation when you're in tune with your curiosity. You just take the next step to find a job that empowers you to follow your passion. It becomes natural to pair your curiosity with a future job and future career once you pair it with a major. You don't want to go through college saying, "I'm curious about this, but I'll wait to pursue it." College is the best time to go for it.

For example, I became interested in entrepreneurship as a pre-law English major in college. I read about it and thought about it, but didn't know if it was something I could do for my career. So I decided to try it by starting a blog (a super low-risk move) my senior year in college called TakeYourSuccess.com. I soon learned that I loved creating content and providing value to people.

I dropped the lawyer idea, and now I'm an author and entrepreneur because I followed my curiosity with small actions over time. And not a day goes by where I don't love my work, which is why I'm always working.

My curiosity turned into my lifelong passion, and it can do the same for you if you are open to giving it a chance. Follow your curiosity, and you won't work another day in your life.

Rule #66 - Pick one focus and master it

Popular opinion says college is the time to try everything. If taken at face value, then sure this statement is fine. But this attitude can also turn into a dangerous, slippery slope where students try to do too much and are mediocre at everything their entire lives. They only scratch the surface and don't achieve what they want in any of their pursuits because they didn't give themselves a chance.

You don't want that. Here's what you want: Find something you're good at and you're interested in during college, then focus on that one area for as long as it takes you to master it.

To find this one focus area, try new things and explore during your first year or two of college. But during the start of sophomore or junior year, decide one area where you're going to lock in and focus. Concentrate your energy and time on this one thing, and you'll eventually master it.

For example, if you know chemistry is your thing by your sophomore year of college, this is a big advantage. Now you can start doing research with a professor. Seek out challenging summer internships to advance your knowledge. Take graduate courses as an undergraduate. Request lab time to test your own hypothesizes and do experiments.

By focusing, you'll make big strides in one subject instead of baby steps in five different subjects. And this will only lead to good things after college.

Rule #67 - Build your personal brand

An established personal brand becomes your most versatile asset when applying for internships, grad schools, or full-time jobs. If you have one, this online presence will be the driving force behind your resume, LinkedIn summary, cover letter, personal statement, and interview answers. If you don't, you're frankly in trouble because it's hard to compete with other college students who have a personal brand.

So how do you get ahead of the competition and build up a strong digital media presence? The next rule is about starting a blog, that's the biggest way. But blogging is not the only avenue to win over the minds of a recruiter who searches your name in Google.

Take advantage of social media. Use your knowledge of Facebook, YouTube, Twitter, Instagram, and LinkedIn to create content that shows your passion, knowledge, and relates to your field. Interview professionals and post it on your LinkedIn page. Do a three-minute YouTube video about why you're excited about your industry.

Follow professionals on Twitter and tweet responses to engage them in conversation.

Companies are not only using online searches to qualify candidates, but they're also recruiting through social media. So instead of making your social media account private to cover up your embarrassing pictures from recruiters, use your social media presence as an advantage to highlight your unique skills. All it takes is one piece of content to get the attention of a hiring manager.

Not many college students think this way about their personal brand and digital networking. When you do, your personal brand becomes a game changer for finding internships, applying to grad school, and getting a full-time job offer, regardless of your field.

Rule #68 - Start a blog

How does doing one activity that will lead you to becoming an expert in a subject, developing your writing skills, learning marketing tactics, gaining wonderful connections, upgrading your resume, and significantly improving your job prospects sound? Oh yeah, I forgot the best part, which is you help a ton of people and often get that warm, fuzzy feeling inside.

You can achieve all of this by doing one thing: starting a blog. That's right. For your personal and professional skills, one of the best moves you can make is to create a website and write content. So if you think blogging is a waste of time that only losers who don't have a job pursue, you're wrong.

A blog becomes a digital resume that showcases your credibility and a positive online presence for the world (job recruiters) to see. You get to control the conversation based on what you write about, meaning you'll make yourself look impressive. Plus, it's not that hard.

Spend around one hour a week writing a blog post about a subject that you want to be seen as an expert in. At the end of a year, you will have 52 pieces of content that all speak toward your knowledge in that subject. That experience is more valuable than the vast majority of internships out there!

I started a blog my senior year of college. Through that blog, I helped a ton of people, decided to write a book, wrote another, and now you're reading my third book.

Where did all this come from? By starting a blog. Did I forecast years into the future knowing I'd be an author and entrepreneur because of it? Not a chance.

This is not to say you need to write books or be an entrepreneur through a blog. It is to say that starting a blog and building a platform opens many doors going forward. And at the least, it's your digital resume that will impress graduate schools and employers.

If you're going into communications, writing, media, or marketing, a blog will be a golden resource in your job search (which reminds me of my first book *The Golden Resume*). If you're in a field that values writing less, creating a blog will help you stand out amongst all the engineers, for example, who speak the same and have the same experiences. It shows you make use of your free time and take initiative.

Lastly, don't worry about not knowing how to get started. You don't need to know how to code or create a website from scratch. You can use wordpress.com or pay around $50 a year (more than worth it at 14 cents a day) for your own site. If you want a specific tutorial, visit TakeYourSuccess.com/why-start-a-blog/ and I'll walk you through what to do. And if you have more questions, you can email brian@takeyoursuccess.com and I'll personally help you with this because I'm a big believer in blogging—it's why I'm here today.

Rule #69 - Make the most of summer

Imagine how two different groups of people spend their summer. One group goes to bed at 4 A.M. and wakes up at noon after watching a full Netflix session in between. Their brains melt because the only productive thing they do all summer break is buy overpriced books for the fall semester. In the other group, they intern at a top company in their field of study and learn more than they could imagine every day at the office. They have fun going to happy hours during the week and catching up with friends during the weekend. They find the perfect balance between having a productive, challenging summer and getting a refreshing break from college classes.

There's a big difference between wasting away during the summer, and wasting no time to excel at life. The top students do the latter. So how do you make the most out of summer? It all starts with early preparation, a plan, and sometimes perseverance.

To find a rewarding summer work experience, set aside a few hours a week in the start of the spring semester to research interesting internships and their application deadlines. The reason I don't recommend starting earlier is because many organizations look to hire full-time positions in the fall and hire interns in the spring. Make a reminder of these application deadlines to be safe because some will creep up before you know it in February or March.

Plan A needs to be finding a paid internship in your field of study. In all but the most obscure fields, there are paid internships across the country that will give you clarity into your future career and pad your bank account. You cross off two birds with one stone.

Plan B is to decide based on your situation whether you want to do an unpaid internship for the experience or take a summer job (nanny, lifeguard, waiter) for the money. Ideally you don't need the money and are on your parents bankroll to pursue your passion during the summer. With this financial backing, you can find a position at a fashion firm, with a professional sports team, or at a music festival company. Seeking unpaid internships can actually open more doors than a paid internship, it just doesn't pay the bills.

If you take the summer job and can't intern in your field, go shadow a professional during the summer. Professionals are always open to talking to a student about their job and career because they've been in your shoes before, it makes them feel important, and they appreciate you taking your future serious. You gain insight into the highs and lows of the job, and get a clearer picture if that's the work you could see yourself doing.

Once you know your Plan A and Plan B, to give yourself the best odds, you'll want to network like a crazy person. Tell your friends and family you're looking for an internship in a certain field, post it in your fraternity's Facebook group, ask your professor for assistance in office hours, utilize career services, and go to on-campus recruiting events. If these contacts don't know someone to help you, the odds are they know someone who does. It's a small world when you cultivate your network and their network. So go all out, and leave no stone unturned.

This is more work than waiting until the semester ends and taking the job that requires the least amount of upfront work, but it's worth it. Because if you waste your summer not doing much, then you'll come back to school having made no progress on where you left off in the spring. But if you take your summer serious, you'll come back to school in the fall with more clarity on whether your major and career path is right for you, gain more work experience, and improve your future prospects.

Rule #70 - Don't end up in online hell

The purpose of this book is to help you get the most out of college. And there are many moves to accomplish that laid out in this book. But a winning strategy covers not only offense, but also defense. And that's why it's crucial in your college experience to protect yourself from a mistake that could ruin your future.

I'm talking about a night where you drink until you're blacked out, mistake a random small business office for your house, and smash through their glass door to pass out on their lobby couch. Once you gain coherence, you're in a jail cell with a felony, a news story mentioning your name, and a mugshot on the first page of Google when your name is searched. (I know someone who actually did this their freshman year of college.)

Another example is you're drunk and start jokingly yelling at someone. A friend records it and posts it online where it's taken as serious. That's only an example, but with access to video in the palm of everyone's hand, one temporary bad decision can haunt you.

Or maybe you post something racist, demeaning, or unfair on one of your social media accounts and it sticks online.

A stupid decision during our parents' and grandparents' time in college would go away. But nowadays a stupid college decision that gets posted to the Internet can gain permanent life.

And this is lethal to a job search. Because you can guarantee that employers and grad schools are searching your name on Google to see what they can find. At that point, any information is fair game. Any inappropriate picture or negative message can make the difference that costs you the job offer or grad school acceptance package.

So keep this in mind during your college years. The last thing you need is to work your butt off for four years and face a tremendous setback from one stupid decision.

College is a blast and you can still have fun and mess around with your friends. Just avoid crossing the line doing something dumb and you will be fine.

PERSONAL DEVELOPMENT

Rule #71 - Get out of your comfort zone

A new place, new friends, and new lifestyle in college will definitely put you out of their comfort zone. However, in a month or two your situation will turn into a familiar routine of walking the same route to class, seeing the same faces, and following the same schedule. The key to overcome a mundane life is to resist complete comfort.

Because you'll find the most rewarding exercise is to intentionally get outside your comfort zone. When you're scared to skydive and then you do it, you realize that all your fear came from your mind. This process of going outside your comfort zone gives you confidence and courage that is worth more than gold.

There is nothing else like it that will improve your character, develop willpower, and unleash your potential to achieve beautiful things in life than leaving your comfort zone. Each time you do this will be challenging, and because of this you grow through it and discover things about yourself. So make it happen by trying new things, doing what scares you, taking risks, challenging yourself, and intentionally doing uncomfortable activities.

You can start small by eating alone in a crowded dining hall or going to the movies alone. Meditate in your dorm room for 15 minutes in the morning. Travel abroad by yourself or go to a new city for the summer and live by yourself. Ask 10 hot girls or guys for their numbers. Climb a mountain.

This might seem a silly exercise in personal development, but it doesn't stop there. Because practicing courage has tangible results in your college and professional life. If you've done stand up comedy in a room full of strangers, then it's easy to give a speech in front of your student organization and run for president. Or if you've sang in a restaurant to your girlfriend, then cold calling employees at the firm you want to work for will be no big deal. Plus, those around you will be contagious to your spirit that's willing to try new things. Doing something even though it's out of your comfort zone will transform your life.

I love what F. Scott Fitzgerald said, "For what it's worth: it's never too late to be whoever you want to be. I hope you live a life you're proud of, and if you find that you're not, I hope you have the strength to start all over again." So if you wish you were more of a risk taker or ambitious, you can become that or whoever you want to be by getting out of your comfort zone.

Rule #72 - Question everything

Up until your college years, you've probably bought into viewpoints popular from your hometown, family, or friends. Now, surrounded by new people, you can question those things you've grown up believing and decide on your own.

To be a successful college student, you may think you'll need to know it all. You'd be better off in college by reverting back to a three-year-old's mindset and question everything with the word why. Let the questions "Why should I think this?" and "Why should I do that?" be at the top of your tongue.

Behind every why, there is a reasonable answer that completely changes how you think about it. And when you ask yourself why you do something, it forces you to evaluate its usefulness and decide whether you want to continue or stop it. These questions lead to positive changes, new beliefs, and increased happiness.

This doesn't mean you take it to the extreme and stop eating to see if you will die (you will die) or attempt to jump off your roof and fly (you probably will die) because you haven't done it before. It does mean you question life's smaller and bigger truths to get away from complacency and establish your core beliefs.

I mentioned questioning your habits, and it's also crucial that you interrogate life's fundamental questions. Question your spirituality. Do you believe in Jesus? Why or why not? Question your political views. Are you a republican, democrat, or have your own beliefs that go beyond conservative and liberal views? Question the government. Question the media. Question the economy. In fact, question this book and me. I'm not infallible. There may be a college rule that you feel I'm completely wrong about.

So if a friend goes against your beliefs, don't immediately disagree with them and raise your voice in protest. Instead of seeing it as a personal attack, see it as an invitation. Honestly look at the issue from their perspective. Listen to what they have to say, then judge it on merit on your own time. Being close minded about something does absolutely nothing for you. There's no shame in being humble enough to change your mind.

Once you answer a question, go on to the next question. Don't stop questioning and life will remain exciting. These questions are your roads to growth and exploration. So what's something you need to start questioning?

Rule #73 - Think big or go home

College students are in the perfect scenario to think big. Your brain is close to fully developed and you still have 60 or more years in front of you to accomplish what you set out to. But so few students decide to think big and instead they practice thinking small at all hours of the day. And by not spending time to think big, you're always going to live small.

Why think big? Consider what happens when you think small. Small thinkers grind away at their to-do list to get everything done, and feel they don't have time to be creative or think with a bigger perspective. They're focused on being efficient, which isn't a bad thing in itself. So they run from class to assignment, complete random tasks like returning books and returning borrowed clothes, and call it a day. They react to life's circumstances as they come. However effective this small mindset is, the bigger problem is it causes your whole life to become a to-do list. Your ultimate achievement is to only cross these small tasks off your list, before you start all over tomorrow. Talk about depressing and living the rat race. Plus, when this mindset is developed in college, it sticks with you or gets worse in your career. You complete your small tasks, but they never end, as life passes you by.

By thinking big, you act ambitious, and live inspired in your pursuit of your journey. Where small thinkers are reactive to life's events, big thinkers are proactive to pursue the day's most valuable activities. Each day has purpose.

Big thinkers are ignorant of the odds because the odds are for spectators. The odds of success don't matter at this point. Let your mind run free with zero limitations to see how far you can get.

For example, how could you create an organization that changes the world on a global scale? What community problem needs to be addressed and how could you find the solution? What's an area you can solve a problem for people and scale it?

When you plant the seeds to think big in college, you cultivate the habit of looking at the big picture and living big in the present to the future. Once you experience the results from thinking big and acting big, you'll see there's no other way to live.

Rule #74 - **Play to your strengths**

Some students are happy with graduating, getting a job, and being in the middle area where they're not struggling but also not excelling in life. Other students have big dreams of being a Fortune 500 CEO, creating their own clothing line, or being a professional actor.

For the big dreamers, the only way you're going to reach your goals and become great is to play to your strengths.

Because focusing on your weaknesses will be far more frustrating, time-consuming, and futile when it comes to results. If you make progress on one of your weaknesses, now you're only average.

However, if you make progress on something you're already skilled at, now you've become great. And when you're great, you can keep going to become elite. Capitalizing on a strength can return results of 10x, 100x, or 1,000x.

How this plays out in college is if you're a talented artist majoring in art, instead of putting in eight hours each week to your biology class and art class, give art 13 hours and biology three hours. A skilled artist who sucks at biology is going to have far more opportunities than an average artist who is decent in biology.

You'll also be far happier during the week when you give the maximum hours to your strengths and do the minimum on your weaknesses. Screw being well-rounded. Instead, invest in your strengths and do the bare minimum on your weaknesses until you have time to develop them.

Rule #75 - Set a long-term goal

Some students have blinders on when it comes to the big picture. They go all out to get a high grade point average because they think that's what will help them. They pick the major they think is the most impressive. But they never set a long-term goal.

When you don't know what you're doing all the work for, it makes everything more difficult.

It's a completely different world for the students who create a long-term goal. They know the mission and why the daily effort is necessary.

With the big picture in mind, you'll have a plan of where you're going and figure it out as you go. Without the big picture in mind, you often end up directionless and confused in school and after.

If you change your long-term goal along the way, that's fine. It wasn't for loss because you established positive habits and now you can use what you learned in this new direction.

Goals take time. But that doesn't mean you should stop exploring routes and avenues to reach your goal.

Write down specifically what you want, why you want it, and how you're going to feel when it happens. Then hold onto that goal and remind yourself of it everyday. Embodying your long-term goal will make it stick in your mind to energize your days with productivity. Psychology has a profound effect on your feelings and performance, so make the most of it by creating a long-term goal.

For example, a student has the long-term goal of becoming a doctor because she remembers how a doctor saved her life when she was a kid and the feeling of a new shot at life. With this in mind, this student knows to become a doctor she needs to go to med school. To get into med school she needs to do well on the MCAT and have a high college GPA.

She worked backwards, so she isn't studying just for her grades. But she's studying with the belief that each achievement gets her a step closer to becoming a doctor.

When you have a long-term goal that you truly want, it makes the moments of drudgery more bearable and the moments when you're on top of the world feel even better. Each class and action has a meaning greater than itself. They all lead to your long-term goal.

Knowing what you want, why you want it, and how you're going to feel when it happens, allows you to work backwards to go from your goal to your present situation. This mentality will lead you to college and career success if you stick with it. Now what's your long-term goal?

Rule #76 - Dress for confidence

Coming from a private high school with mandatory dress codes, I first loved the idea of wearing whatever I wanted to my college classes. On the first day of class, my excitement disappeared. I realized picking out clothes every morning would be a problem. And since wearing the same thing each day is social suicide, I already missed the mandatory dress code.

Why does what you wear to class matter? We judge people based on what they wear. You do it, so you better believe other people do it to you. So one reason to dress well to class is to present yourself in a positive light.

But here's the main reason. When you wake up in time to shower, brush your teeth, and dress nice, you gain energy and confidence to tackle the day. It's the concept of look good, feel good, and perform at your best.

And the opposite effect happens when you roll out of bed and go to class in your pajamas. Good luck staying awake and focusing when you're dressed for a nap. Having the freedom to dress like you slept in a ditch doesn't mean you should do it.

Getting a few key essentials in your wardrobe makes it easy to dress for confidence. Jeans and shorts (not cargo shorts), quality t-shirts, and some nice sandals, gym shoes, or boots is all you need to mix and match. Just keep in mind, most people don't dress up a ton for class.

In addition to classes, you also want to be prepared for campus interviews. Buy one nice, fitted suit that you can rely on during your college career. Black is always a solid choice.

You don't need a personal shopper or to be decked out in designer apparel from head to toe. You just want to find your own style, and make a good impression. I'm no fashionista, but I think it makes a difference.

Rule #77 - Read 20 minutes a day

The majority of students don't like the idea of reading, because it reminds them of studying. Reading becomes busy work instead of an adventure. However, please don't let school reading give you a sour taste for personal reading. Why? Because reading develops greater productivity and focus, improves writing and speaking skills, allows your body to release stress, aids memory, and makes falling asleep easier when you pick up a book before bed. Reading about other people's successes and failures gives you wisdom, inspiration, and goals. You learn what interests you and what you want in life. You learn random fun facts. What does reading not do?

Most importantly, I bet there's a book out there with a solution to 99% of your problems. Are you nervous about speaking in front of your student organization, do you not know how to eat healthy, or are you feeling down on life? Read a book on public speaking, health and nutrition, or the power of positive thinking.

Do you want to be more knowledgeable about a subject than anyone you know? Read 10 books on this subject and you'll be on your way.

Authors have done all the research and work to master the problems you're facing, all you need to do is read their book. Use reading, a skill you learned in kindergarten, to transform your life.

And if you don't have 20 minutes a day to read, then that's a sign you don't have a life. Come on, it's only 20 minutes. Read a book instead of watching a show, read before bed, or read while walking to class—I don't care. You might not look cool, but the benefits from reading will be worth it.

Grab a book each day to massage your mind, body, and soul. I promise reading will be the best 20-minute investment you make each day.

Rule #78 - Go to the big guest lectures

Kanye West gave a guest lecture at Oxford University. Stephen King addressed English majors at the University of Massachusetts. Oprah Winfrey taught at Stanford University. Not every school has the prestige or connections to attract celebrities like these, but the point is that experts in all fields visit college campuses to guest lecture.

And it's a no brainer to attend these lectures open to your entire school, department, or class. You won't get this same access after you graduate.

These intelligent, crafty speakers can light a fire in you to push you out of a rut or to take your passion to the next level. Because of their vast experience, they will offer a new point of view that rocks your perspective. A night with a notable guest speaker can energize, motivate, and sustain your dreams more than 15 weeks with your normal professor.

That's why the reward of gaining life-changing inspiration or clarity is worth the risk of not getting as much out of it as you wanted—or being bored. You never know when you're going to strike gold. It only takes one guest lecture to open your eyes to a new world of possibility.

For the reader who is a devil's advocate and says you don't need to go because you can always watch it later on YouTube, I have two things to say. One, sometimes these lectures are exclusive to the live audience and won't be published online. Two, your body doesn't get filled with the same inspiring energy and attention when you're watching online eating Doritos compared to being there in the flesh. Seeing, listening, and breathing the same air as a world-changer does something to your psyche and gives you more passion for your pursuits. Plus, there's no chance of hitting the jackpot and getting your specific question answered if you're viewing from your laptop.

So trust me and go to the live event for an invaluable educational and inspirational moment. Listening to a big name guest lecturer could be the spark for your career that gets you the guest lecturer invite years down the road.

Rule #79 - Keep the college lifestyle in perspective

The college lifestyle is a double-edge sword. It's really fun, but it can be dangerous if you have too much fun.

Take the students who are addicted to the college lifestyle and overdo it. They go out to the bars every night, attend classes only one day a week, and see how high they can get the night they're supposed to study for an exam. This lifestyle is a rush, but it doesn't come on its own. It also brings the demise of their grades, physical health, or mental health. Sometimes heavy consequences follow like academic suspension, lost scholarships, Greek life suspension, and feeling lost without a true purpose. What they sought as an enjoyable time came back to bite them.

These headache situations are their own doing. Avalanches of problems grow when students devote all their time to living it up. And these same students face the hardest time transitioning from college to post-grad life because they put all their eggs in the college basket and then it's over. They don't have much to show for it as everyone else is moving on and they're directionless.

On the other hand, the smart students keep a healthy balance with the college lifestyle. They take advantage of the freedom to go out on a Tuesday night for margaritas, but take care of their business during the rest of the week. Or they sleep in on Saturday without an alarm because they are ahead of their classes. And when post-grad life comes, they get the high-paying jobs in the city of their choice. They didn't get trapped by the college lifestyle. They built solid habits to serve them after graduation.

With this rule I promise I'm not trying to be a fun-sucker. I'm actually aiming to be a fun-promoter. Because the students who maintain balance have more fun during their four years. By keeping this lifestyle in perspective, they get the perks without having to deal with the harsh consequences of falling too in love with this lifestyle.

The reality is that the college lifestyle goes away whether you like it or not. By keeping this way of life in perspective, you'll be happier in college, transition smoother to post-grad, and have more promising opportunities. Those are facts!

Rule #80 - Do what you love

College is a time filled with laughter, tears, love, sadness, joy, despair, and memories. But eventually the college experience ends. Your time as a college student is finite.

Because of this reality, it's critical that you choose the right journey after graduation. The wrong journey is to settle for a job that you don't mind out of school. Life is too short to do this. Settle now, at age 22, and you risk never doing what you love. Don't be an accountant who should have become a singer, or a singer who should have been an accountant.

Instead, do what you love now. When you do what you love, you wake up each and every morning excited to make progress. It's the work that gets you going like nothing else. You lose track of time because you're so engaged in it. How much money you make is always secondary to what you do (although many people make a ton of money working on what they love because they spend the time it takes to master it).

Look for what you love during college in your classes, extracurriculars, readings, videos, guest speakers, side projects, movies, and internships. Take action to try new things. Be open to finding new passions. I promise it's out there. And once you find what you love to do, never let it go. Continue to pursue it until the day you die.

Doing what you love is the key to college success above all else. Find what you love doing and you've won. Don't do what you love, and you've lost.

It might be ironic that I end a college success book with not college advice, but life advice. I've found that if you do what you love, you'll find more happiness and success than you could dream about. That's how to college and how to live. Now close this book and get after it!

Special Request

Thank you for spending the time to read my book! I hope you got a ton of value out of it.

Getting feedback is one of my favorite things because it helps me improve and makes the next version of this book better. That's why I really appreciate hearing what you have to say.

Please leave me a helpful review on Amazon letting me know what you thought of the book.

I appreciate you!
- Brian Robben

About The Author

Brian Robben is the three-time author of *The Golden Resume*, *Freedom Mindset*, and *How To College*.

Robben is also the founder and writer at TakeYourSuccess.com—which helps college students make the most of their college experience through time-management systems, study strategies, and career advice.

He is 23 years old and currently lives in Cincinnati, Ohio. Find out more about him at TakeYourSuccess.com

More From Brian Robben

Are you struggling to write a successful resume? Are you frustrated with applying to organizations and not getting interviews? Or maybe you are getting interviews, but you struggle to interview well and ultimately get rejected.

No matter your situation, *The Golden Resume* will show you how to get the big internship or job you desire and deserve, through mastering your resume and acing interviews.

What Brian Robben shares in these pages are the proven strategies that the top-performers and Brian utilized to dominate the job search.

The Golden Resume has been created to give you resume and interview essentials in a concise and applicable format that step-by-step teaches you:

- Insight into recruiters and hiring manager's mindset

- Why most resumes are ignored

- How to make your resume stand out for limitless job interviews

- The ways to craft your digital identity and online footprint

- The secrets to acing interviews and being an unforgettable candidate

- One final job search essential to enhance your success

Order your copy of *The Golden Resume* at amazon.com/author/brianrobben.

Once you get the job you want and the paycheck that comes with it, learn how to master your money with *Freedom Mindset*.

There are two different ways to manage your money and live. Most young adults use their money the wrong way. They work at jobs they don't enjoy. Buy things that don't make them happy in the long term. And are forced to work until they're 65.

Brian Robben's *Freedom Mindset* shows the other way to live. This is a step-by-step guide on how to become rich so you have the freedom to live more and work less.

Robben uncovers:

- Eight Steps To Salary Negotiation Excellence

- The most important factor to becoming rich

- How to destroy debt and stay out of debt

- Your current saving problem and what to do instead

- How to escape the rat race and retire decades early

- The truths and the lies about investing

- A winning investment strategy you can set on autopilot

If you're willing to handle your money differently than most people, this guide will put you on the fast track to get rich and reach financial freedom.

Can you afford not to get this book and lose the opportunity to master your income?

You can get your copy of *Freedom Mindset* at amazon.com/author/brianrobben.

Made in the USA
Middletown, DE
21 June 2019